OPTION STRATEGIES FOR SOPHISTICATED TRADERS

TRADERS PRESS, INC.®
PO Box 6206
GREENVILLE, SC 29606

SERVING TRADERS SINCE 1975
HTTP://WWW.TRADERSPRESS.COM

MITCH CRASK

ISBN: 0-934380-96-1
Published by: Traders Press, Inc.®

This publication is designed to provide accurate and authoritative information with regard to the subject matter covered. It is sold with the understanding that the publisher is not engaged in rendering legal, accounting, or other professional advice. If legal advice or other expert assistance is required, the services of a competent professional person should be sought.

Disclaimer

The sole purpose of the statements and illustrations in this book is to provide basic information about investing. No trading, investment or other advice, suggestion or recommendation of any kind is intended, or is being made. If you wish to receive trading or investment advice or recommendations, you should retain the services of a licensed professional. The author is not an investment advisor, broker-dealer or other professional securities institution. It is understood that the author may currently own or, from time to time in the future, own equities, indices, or derivatives used for educational purposes. It is further understood that no claim of gains is made by the author and that, accordingly, no monies should be put at risk unless the total amount put at risk can be lost without materially affecting the life style of the investor. It is further understood that, except for Traders Press and SFO magazine, neither the author nor any of his duly authorized representatives and/or assigns have received, or have agreements to receive at any time in the future, compensation in any form whatsoever from any of the organizations, equities, or services mentioned.

Editing, Layout and Cover Design
by: Teresa Darty Alligood
Editor and Graphic Designer
Traders Press, Inc.®

Traders Press, Inc.®
PO Box 6206
Greenville, SC 29606
Serving Traders Since 1975
http://www.traderspress.com

Dedicated to my wife Patricia, my son Gregory,
my daughter Pam, and my grandchildren,
Erin, Brian, Lisa and Brian.

Acknowledgements

First, I would like to thank Ed Dobson of Traders Press for his patient advice and for steering me to knowledgeable people while this book was being written. Next, I would like to thank Teresa Darty Alligood and Linda Smith of Traders Press. Teresa patiently edited the material I provided her and designed the cover. Linda was the first person I met at the booth at the Chicago Trader's Expo and passed me on to Ed. I would also like to acknowledge the anonymous reviewer, as well as, Gail Osten and Kira McCaffrey Brecht of SFO for publishing the article from which this book sprang. The web site and people at the One Chicago single stock futures exchange were instrumental in providing data and insights that helped draw out many of the examples in this book. Of particular help was a meeting during the early stages of preparation with Peter Borish, Christopher Krohn, Melissa Rios, and Mary Haffenberg of One Chicago. I would also like to thank Chuck Bohm and Tom Frankel of Man Financial for explaining the brokerage house considerations of using a future to cover a short option, especially as related to single stock futures and equity options. Without this information the Switch Trade would be a nice theoretical construct which could not be traded. Finally, I would like to thank my wife who put up with Saturday, Sunday and late night writing sessions. Finally, although I received help from many people, responsibility for the end product is mine alone.

Publisher's Foreword

The wide array of option strategies which may be used to implement virtually any market opinion, and to fine tune one's risk and potential return for that opinion, has always fascinated me. I've studied closely the works available from well known options educators such as Larry McMillan, David Caplan, and George Fontanills.

It was my pleasure and privilege to meet Mitch Crask, the author of this book, at the Traders Expo in Chicago in summer of 2003. It became apparent early into a discussion of option strategies with Mitch that he, too, was not only an avid student of all the strategies that had been written about before, but that he had some pretty interesting ideas of his own, which he sets forth in this book. And the really neat thing about Mitch is that he is no ivory tower theorist…he practices what he preaches, and on a serious scale. In common parlance, he "walks the walk," not just "talks the talk."

It is my hope that this book will serve to expand your knowledge of options strategies and provide the food for thought that will lead to increased profits in your own trading.

Edward Dobson, President   May 6, 2005
Traders Press, Inc.®
Greenville, SC

CHAPTER ONE

OVERVIEW

OPTION STRATEGY APPLICABLE TO STOCKS AND EURODOLLARS

This book presents a strategy combining two derivatives to increase the profitability of option debit spreads. The strategy is called a switch spread because one of the option positions is replaced, or switched, with a futures contract. The switch spread is an option strategy using the basic concepts, outlooks, and strategies of an option debit spread or straddle. Each option strategy is explained in detail. Therefore, if an investor is willing to take the time to carefully work through each example, a working knowledge of options, although useful, is not necessary. Relevant references on options, futures, single stock futures and other derivatives are provided at the end of each chapter. A complete reference section is provided at the end of the book.

Single stock futures are used as examples because there is a price history that permits the use of actual prices rather than theoretical situations. However, as can be seen from part of an August 3, 2004 statement from the Chicago Mercantile Exchange (CME) website (www.cme.com), the same switch spreads could be constructed based on Eurodollars.

CHICAGO, August 3, 2004 — Chicago Mercantile Exchange, Inc. (CME), the largest U.S. futures exchange, yesterday launched its enhanced options system for electronic Eurodollars, combining committed market making, indicative quotes, complex spread combinations and electronic request for quote (e-RFQ) functions. The new state-of-the-art electronic options functionality for Eurodollars will facilitate trading of complex combination and spread trades typically used with short-term interest rate options on futures, within a fully transparent and competitive execution environment.

In the first day of trading using the new options functionality CME reported the following:

- More than 22,000 contracts traded via this new functionality, along with nearly 10,000 Eurodollar options contracts traded on GLOBEX®;
- The new functionality represented approximately 6.0% of the exchange's total Eurodollar options volume of 373,310;
- There were 307 e-RFQs (www.cme.com/edge) and 89 executed trades;
- Ninety percent of eligible users logged into the system; and,
- The majority of volume (nearly 90%) represented trades that were multi-legged, complex spread strategies, including straddles, vertical call spreads, vertical put spreads, call butterflies (3 legs), call condors (4 legs), call "Christmas" trees (3 legs) and call 1x2's ratio spreads.

1

The ability to construct a switch spread is relatively recent. A switch spread requires an underlying instrument with futures and options which have liquidity, committed market making and the possibility of complex spread combinations based on net debit and net credit orders. Two current possibilities in the United States are single stock futures (One Chicago) and Eurodollars (The Chicago Mercantile Exchange). On January 29, 2000 the London International Financial Futures and Options Exchange (LIFFE) began trading futures on individual stocks. Internationally, London remains the most active area offering the three requisite criteria for switch trades. Single stock futures began trading in the United State in early 2001. I am often asked where to find brokers who will take a switch trade. A good source is "Active Trader's Online Brokerage Guide" [2004]. <u>Active Trader.</u> 5, 10, 28-41. (October).

Readers unfamiliar with any of the terms in this book are referred to the Glossary in Appendix A. To ensure correctness, the words "stock" and "option" need to be explained. The meaning of the word "stock" is restricted to common stocks that have all three characteristics listed below:
- stocks listed on a major stock exchange,
- stocks with listed options on a major option exchange, and
- stocks with single stock futures listed on a major single stock futures exchange.
  The term "major exchange" is not restricted to exchanges located in the United   States.

Although there are many types of options, including commodity options and futures options, the term "options" is restricted to stock options that are listed on a major exchange. The term "major exchange" is not restricted to exchanges located in the United States. Unless specifically stated the word "option" refers to an American style option as opposed to a European style option. An American style option can be exercised by the holder at any time between purchase and expiration. A European style option may be exercised only on its expiration date.

THE SWITCH SPREAD STRATEGY DEFINED

The basic strategy is called a "switch" spread because it switches a debit spread or straddle into a credit position by switching some or all of the long options in debit spreads to single stock futures. As a result, the option debit spread changes to a credit position automatically increasing profit potential and improving the reward/risk ratio. The advantage of a credit spread is you can be wrong and still make money. This is not true with a debit spread. Disadvantages of using switch spreads include the increased margin requirement of the switch credit spread compared to the equivalent option debit position. As a result, some of the switch strategies may be unacceptable for investors unwilling to post the additional margin required for the single stock future. Another disadvantage is the sometimes unlimited potential loss that must be managed through position management considerations.

Although this is not a book on single stock futures, certain characteristics of single stock futures and how they differ from the characteristics of stocks and options are important. These differences form the basis for all switch strategies. The relevant differences are provided below. These characteristics are included as Appendix B because they are repeatedly referenced throughout.

SIMILARITIES AND DIFFERENCES BETWEEN OPTIONS, STOCKS AND FUTURES

The following characteristics are relevant to switch strategies. Option and stock characteristics that are different from futures contracts are in bold.

- The buyer of an option has the right to demand delivery of the underlying stock anytime before the expiration date. The same is true for a futures contract.
- **The buyer of a futures contract has the obligation to take delivery of the underlying at expiration.** The option purchaser does not have this obligation.
- For a limited period of time, the sale of an option contract creates an obligation to deliver the underlying upon demand. The same is true for a futures contract.
- **A future is considered at "fair value" when its price is consistent with the theoretical formula:**
  Fair Value = Stock Price x (1 + annualized interest rate - dividend).
- **For a futures contract, the market price and the theoretical price are usually very close to one another.** All of the variables in the formula for the price of a futures contract are a question of fact and can be determined. Therefore, when a futures contract is not at or near the fair market value, either wait for arbitrage to correct the situation or check the assumptions about either the interest rate or the dividends. This is not the case for options. Theoretical prices and market prices are often different because the option pricing formula has one variable, volatility of the underlying, which can be estimated in a statistical probability sense only.
- Both implied volatility and the volatility of the underlying have a major impact on the price of an option. **The term implied volatility has no meaning in relation to the price of a futures contract because the volatility of the underlying has no impact on the price of a futures contract.** (See the formula for the fair market value of a futures contract.)
- Time decay can become a major consideration for some option spreads. **A futures contract does not experience time decay.** (See the formula for the fair market value of a futures contract.)
- **Once the fair value is determined, the future has a delta close to or equal to 1.0.**
- **A futures contract can be shorted on a down tick. A stock cannot.**
- **A future can be shorted without borrowing the stock. A stock cannot.**
- **A single stock future has a twenty percent margin requirement.** Compare this to stocks with a twenty-five percent margin for pattern day traders and a fifty percent margin requirement for trades that are open more than one day.
- For any given underlying security, there are option alternatives with different strike prices and different expiration dates. **There may be futures contracts with different expiration dates, however, the prices are usually close to the underlying price and for each expiration date there is only one price, the fair value.**
- **Shorting a futures contract does not create a credit to your account.**

The key to the switch strategy is three of the differences between options and single stock futures.

- A single stock future price is not related to the volatility of the underlying stock.
- A single stock future does not experience time decay.
- In most cases, once the Fair Value is determined, a single stock future has a Delta at, or very close to 1.00.

All factors in the futures pricing formula are known. The one unknown in the option pricing formula is volatility. This makes volatility a key element in the price of an option. In fact, many traders believe a thorough understanding of volatility is the most essential factor in creating profitable option trades. Because switch trades have option positions as a major component, an understanding of volatility is critical to creating and executing profitable switch trades. Therefore, a brief explanation of volatility seems in order. Readers familiar with the role volatility plays in investing and the implications for options and futures can skip the brief comments on volatility and volatility skews.

VOLATILITY

Technical analysis uses the term volatility in four ways

- historical volatility,
- implied volatility,
- volatility skews and
- expected or forecast volatility

For a thorough explanation of volatility and its relationship to option strategies see Fontanills and Gentile[2003] and McMillan[2002].

HISTORICAL VOLATILITY ~ Historical volatility is a statistical probability statement about how much a stock price has fluctuated over a specified period of time in the past. Volatility is used to estimate the price range of future stock prices because it is a statistical measurement of the past performance of the price of a stock (usually the close) over a specified period of time.

Stated in words, historical volatility measures the probability that a particular stock will make large percentage movements in the future based on price movements over a specific period of time in the past. Mathematically, historical volatility is defined as the annualized standard deviation of the percentage moves of the underlying stock price over a specified period of time.

The main causes of high volatility are:

- the arrival of new information,
- unforeseen events,
- a period where major stocks and stock indexes make consistently large percentage moves over a relatively extended period of time,
- approaching corporate earnings reports, and
- situations where emotions begin driving trading decisions.

New information includes interest rate changes, changes in the economy such as consumer spending intentions, proposed tax changes, proposed government regulations, anticipated actions by government regulatory agencies such as anticipated approval of a new pharmaceutical by the Food and Drug Administration (FDA) and corporate announcements such as a proposed merger or stock split. These factors, taken as a group, increase the potential for assertive buying and selling. Unforeseen events include occurrences as diverse as the million dollar spilled-coffee award sustained by McDonalds™ and 9/11. When investors are caught unaware, the market usually moves violently up or down. Sometimes it moves in both directions at the same time because unforeseen news creates uncertainty which forces investors to re-evaluate their expectations. A period where major stocks and stock indexes make consistently large percentage moves over a relatively extended period of time, such as the long-term bear market that began in March, 2000, creates uncertainty on the part of investors. It is generally agreed that most options experience increased volatility as the date for company quarterly or annual earning reports approach. Finally, trading related situations, such as the panic of October, 1987, create uncertainty and fear. When such emotions begin driving investment decisions, volatility usually goes through the roof. An important point to remember is that volatility does not help predict the direction of the market or the direction of an individual stock. It simply indicates the potential extent of an anticipated move with the direction uncertain.

Option sellers demand more money for an option on a stock that has the ability to make large percentage moves in a relatively short period of time. The additional premium is needed to offset the higher risk of being exercised. Likewise, buyers will be willing to pay more for an option because there is a greater chance of the option becoming profitable. Therefore, an option on a stock with a high volatility has a higher premium than an option on a stock with a low volatility.

Historical volatility is applied to the underlying stock. Therefore, anytime you see the term volatility applied to a stock, unless otherwise stated, historical volatility is being used. Implied volatility relates to options and is used to explain the difference between the value that the market places on an option and the theoretical price of the option.

IMPLIED VOLATILITY ~ Implied volatility is a computed value that matches the theoretical price of an option with its current market price. The best known option pricing model is the Black-Scholes model. An excellent, simple, easy to understand visual presentation of Black-Scholes in PowerPoint® format is provided by Marlow[2001]. Six factors are used to calculate an option price:
- the underlying stock price,
- striking price of the option,
- time to expiration,
- risk-free interest rate,
- dividends and
- volatility of the underlying stock.

All of the factors except volatility are fixed. Therefore, it is assumed that any difference between an option's current market value and its theoretical value (calculated using historical volatility) is because the market is using a different value for volatility. The different value for volatility is called implied volatility and is a calculated figure arising from the current market price of the option. In other words, implied volatility represents market expectations regarding the future volatility of the underlying stock. Looked at another way, implied volatility is the collective wisdom of the market about the future volatility of the underlying as it relates to an option with a specific strike price and expiration date. As a result, option prices often have a higher or lower implied volatility than the historical volatility of the underlying stock. In summary, historical volatility is calculated using known past prices of the underlying stock while implied volatility is derived and reflects the collective market expectations about the magnitude, direction and timing of future price moves of the underlying stock.

This means each option has its own, individual, implied volatility. For example, if the market expects a large movement in the price of the underlying to begin six months from now, the shorter-term options will have less implied volatility than the longer-term options. Likewise, if the market expects the underlying to move five points and then stop, options that are greater than five points out-of-the-money will have a lower implied volatility than options on the same underlying that are five points or less out-of-the-money. This creates a situation called a volatility skew.

VOLATILITY SKEWS ~ A volatility skew exists when two or more options with either different strikes and/or different expiration dates have significant differences in their implied volatilities. Under certain circumstances, a volatility skew can create an attractive switch trade. To illustrate, take a bull call debit spread (Chapter Nine) where the lower strike has a higher implied volatility than the higher strike option on the same underlying. The basic assumption of the bull call debit spread is that the higher premium paid for the long option with high volatility is offset by the higher premium received from the sale of the higher strike option. This assumption does not hold for a situation where there is a volatility skew and the lower strike option has significantly greater implied volatility than the higher strike option. Switching a long single stock future for the long lower strike option with the higher implied volatility offers an opportunity to create a position with a higher profit potential and improved breakeven point than the equivalent bull call debit option spread.

Sophisticated options traders are continually looking forward and attempting to forecast the future volatility of a stock. The option trader examines historical volatility over different time periods to help determine the future or expected volatility of the underlying at some future point in time. There is, of course, no way to know for sure. However, some help is provided by the fact that historical volatility and implied volatility are cyclical in nature. Option traders often refer to an option as "over-priced" or "underpriced." This represents a value judgment based upon the individual trader's assessment of the expected future volatility of the underlying stock compared to the current implied volatility.

EXPECTED VOLATILITY ~ Expected volatility is the forecast of an individual investor, and, as such, represents an individual investor's expectations about future volatility. This value is based on the analysis of an individual investor. It may or may not equal either historical or implied volatility.

Because historical volatility is a statistical measure, it has clearly stated statistical margins of error. Implied volatility is a value derived from the current price of an option. Implied volatility represents the aggregate market opinion about the future volatility of a stock within a given price range within a given time frame. However, expected volatility is highly subjective. It is only as good as the person making the estimates. Historical and implied volatility are important to understanding and using switch spreads.

IMPACT OF VOLATILITY ON THE SWITCH SPREAD

The impact of volatility is best illustrated when a long single stock future is switched for a long option. Because the price of the single stock future is not based on the volatility of the underlying stock, you avoid paying the high premium on the purchased call option portion of the spread; however, you still receive the high premium from the sale of the short call. This results in six advantages for the switch strategy:

- Greater profit potential.
- Risk management is easier because the switch spread is profitable over a greater price range.
- Time decay is not a factor.
- High volatility stocks provide greater profit potential.
- Volatility skews toward the long leg have no affect on profitability.
- Under certain circumstances, an option with a low implied volatility can offer attractive profit potential.

TIME DECAY

The longer an option has to expiration, the more time it has to increase or decrease in value. Therefore, at any given stock price, a long-term option sells for more than a short-term option. Furthermore, an option's time value decreases to zero at expiration. This is called time decay. The rate of time decay is related to the square root of the time remaining. This means an option's time value decreases slowly at first and then time value loss rapidly accelerates as the expiration date approaches. Because of the mathematics of the curvilinear function, the rate of rapidly increasing time loss begins at about eight weeks. However, the value of a single stock future is not a function of time to expiration. Therefore, a single stock future does not experience time decay. This means switch spreads become attractive alternatives for option spread strategies such as the calendar spread.

DELTA

Delta is a measure of how much the price of an option changes when the price of the underlying changes by one dollar. Technically speaking, Delta is the first partial derivative of the price of an option as it is related to the price of the underlying over time. When the strike price is far above the stock price, the premium is relatively low and the volatility and time factors have little impact. This is important for three reasons:

- The closer the stock price is to the strike price, the more the option costs which means more money into your account from selling, or going short, the option.
- The single stock future has a delta equal or close to 1.0. For many spreads, such as the vertical debit call spread, this makes the delta of the short call work in your favor.
- The time value premium is greatest when the stock price and the strike price are the same. Therefore, switching a single stock future for a long at-the-money or slightly in-the-money option permits going short an option that is closer to the money. This increases the credit by increasing the time value component of the short option price.

DIFFERENT FROM MATCHED-PAIRS FUTURES TRADES

The switch strategy is different from a popular futures trading strategy called matched-pairs trading. Matched-pairs trading refers to going long one single stock future and short a related single stock future in the same industry (for example, long a Coke single stock future and short a Pepsi single stock future). This strategy is based on statistical relationships between the prices of the two stocks. The switch strategy is based on the price of an option and the price of a single stock future on the same underlying stock. However, under certain conditions, futures traders could use the switch strategy as an alternative to matched-pairs trading when matched-pairs trading is considered inappropriate because of statistical considerations.

CONCLUSION

A new investment strategy called a switch spread is defined as a strategy that turns a debit spread into a credit spread by switching one of the long option legs of a debit spread with a long single stock future. A switch spread works because of differences between how volatility, volatility skews, time decay and delta affect the switch spread. The usefulness of the switch strategy is based on the fact that the price of a single stock future does not depend on volatility and the single stock future does not experience time decay. A brief overview of historical, implied and expected volatility is provided. The impact of volatility, volatility skews, time decay and delta on the switch spread is also drawn out.

Switch spreads have the following advantages over their equivalent debit option spreads:
- Greater profit potential.
- Risk management is easier because the switch spread is profitable over a greater price range.
- Time decay is not a factor.
- High volatility stocks provide greater profit potential.
- Volatility skews toward the long leg have no affect on profitability.
- Under certain circumstances, an option with a low implied volatility can offer attractive profit potential.

Switch spreads have two main disadvantages:
- There is sometimes unlimited potential loss that must be managed through position management considerations.
- The margin requirements of a switch spread are usually higher than the equivalent option spread. This is the result of the twenty percent margin required for a single stock future.

REFERENCES

OPTIONS, FUTURES, SINGLE STOCK FUTURES AND OTHER DERIVATIVES

Allure, Marc [2003]. *The Option Strategist.* New York: McGraw-Hill.

Angell, George. [1983]. *Sure Thing Options Trading.* New York: Penguin Group.

Ansbacher, Max [2000]. *The New Options Market 4th Edition.* New York: John Wiley & Sons.

Apostolou, Nick and Barbara Apostolou [2000]. *Keys to Investing in Options and Futures 3rd Edition.* Hauppauge, NY: Barron's Press.

Bernstein, Jake [2003]. *How to Trade the New Single Stock Futures.* Chicago: Dearborn Trade Publishing.

Bigalow, Steve W. [2004]. *Market Timing with Candlesticks. Technical Analysis of Stocks and Commodities,* 22, 5, pp. 88-90.

Bigalow, Steven W. [2002]. *Profitable Candlestick Trading.* New York: John Wiley & Sons.

Brach, Marion A. [2003]. *Real Options in Practice.* New York: John Wiley & Sons.
 Different viewpoint on volatility, time decay and option pricing models such as Black-Scholes. Traders familiar with mathematical game theory and binomial decision trees will find this a must read for an alternative approach to option pricing.

Bittman, James B. [1997]. *Options for the Stock Investor.* New York: McGraw-Hill.

Caplan, David L [1995]. *The New Options Advantage (Revised Edition.)* New York: McGraw-Hill.

Copeland, Tom and Vladimir Antikarov [2001]. *Real Options: A Practical Guide.* New York: Texere, LLC.
 For advanced traders only. Simple algebra and bi-nodal decision trees combined with present value and Bayesian analysis. If you do not have a good understanding of the terms in the previous sentence, then this book is not for you. For people who are comfortable with these concepts, this is an excellent book...a must have.

Crask, Mitch [2004]. *Reply to Margin Question [Crask 2003] In Your Letters. Stocks, Futures, Options,* 3, 2 (February), p.12.
 First use of the term switch spread. Explains the difference between a margin requirement and net debit for a debit spread.

Crask, Mitch [2003]. *Single Stock Futures Add a New Twist to Options Play. Stocks, Futures, Options,* 2, 11 (November), pp. 42-46.

Dicks, James [2004]. *FOREX Made Easy: 6 Ways to Trade the Dollar.* New York: McGraw-Hill.
 Excellent introduction to trading currencies.

Eng, William F. [1988]. *Technical Analysis of Stocks, Options and Futures.* New York: McGraw-Hill.

Evans, Richard E. [2000]. *The Index Fund Solution.* New York: Simon & Schuster.

Ferri, Richard A. [200]. *All about Index Funds.* New York: McGraw-Hill

Fine, Robert E. and Robert B. Feduniak [1988]. *Futures Trading: Concepts and Strategies.* New York: New York Institute of Finance.

Fontanills, George A. [1998]. *The Options Course.* New York: John Wiley & Sons.
 Excellent introduction to options. Clearly written in small, easy-to-learn steps.

Fontanills, George A. [1998]. *The Options Course Workbook: Step-By-Step Exercises and Tests to Help You Master the Options Course.* New York: John Wiley & Sons.
 The title says it all. An excellent workbook that teaches you how to apply the concepts in the companion text.

Gallacher, William R. [1999]. *The Options Edge.* New York: McGraw-Hill.
   A book for intermediate and above option traders.
Gidel, Susan A. [2000]. *Stock Index Futures and Options.* New York: John Wiley & Sons.
Greenberg, Steven A. [2001]. *Single Stock Futures: The Complete Guide.* Greenville, SC: Traders Press, Inc.
Hull, John G. [2003]. *Options, Futures and Other Derivatives 5th Edition.* New York: Prentice-Hall.
   No prior knowledge of options, futures, and swaps. Requires quantitative skills.
Isaacman, Max [2000]. *How to Be an Index Investor.* New York: McGraw-Hill.
Jenkins, Michael S. [1992]. *The Geometry of Stock Market Profits.* Greenville, SC: Traders Press, Inc.
   Chapter Nine on options is one of the best discussions available on the practical aspects of trading options.
Lafferty, Patrick [2002]. *Single Stock Futures.* New York: McGraw-Hill.
Lerman, David. [2001]. *Exchange Traded Funds and the E-mini Stock Index Futures.* New York: John Wiley & Sons.
Lofton, Todd [2001]. *Getting Started in Futures 4th Edition.* New York: John Wiley & Sons.
McClatchy, Will [2003]. *Index Funds.* New York: John Wiley & Sons.
McClean, William [2003]. *Timing Events with the Calendar Spread."* Active Trader, 9, 10 (October), pp. 66-67.
McMillan, Lawrence G. [2002]. *Options as a Strategic Investment. 4th Edition.* New York: New York Institute of Finance.
   The acknowledged guru on options. The Bible on options. If you buy, read and understand only one book on options, this should be the one.
McMillan, Lawrence G. [2002]. *Profit with Options.* New York: John Wiley & Sons.
McMillan, Lawrence G. [1996]. *McMillan on Options.* New York: John Wiley & Sons.
Marlow, Jerry [2001]. *Option Pricing: Black-Scholes Made Easy.* New York: John Wiley & Sons.
   An excellent, simple, easy to understand visual presentation of Black-Scholes in PowerPoint® format. An interactive, animated, option pricing tutorial on CD ROM is included.
Mendoza, Alex [2004]. *Put/Call Parity. Technical Analysis of Stocks and Commodities.* 27, 6 (June), pp. 64.66.
Options Institute, The (Ed.) [1999]. *Options: Essential Concepts & Trading Strategies 3rd Edition.* New York: McGraw-Hill.
   How market makers trade pp. 253-273. The predictive power of options pp. 357-388.
Roth, Harrison [1994]. *LEAPS.* Chicago: Irwin.
   Covers equity options over a period of one to three years.
Seyler, Jeffrey P. [2004]. *Better Returns with Single Stock Futures. Technical Analysis of Stocks and Commodities,* 22, 5 (May), pp. 84-86.
Summa, John F. and Jonathan W. Lubow [2002]. *Options on Futures.* New York: John Wiley & Sons.
   A how-to guide for options on futures. Each strategy is explained with hypothetical examples and reconstruction of actual trades.
Taylor, France [2000]. *Mastering Derivative Markets 2nd Edition.* New York: Prentice-Hall.

Trester, Kenneth R. [2002]. *The Complete Options Player 4th Edition.* Lake Tahoe, NY: Institute for Options Research.

Veale, Stuart R. [2001]. *Stocks, Bonds, Options, Futures 2nd Edition.* New York: New York Institute of Finance.
> Excellent overview of derivatives mentioned in title. Also includes trade execution, back office operations and global investing.

Wasendorf, Russell [2004]. *The Complete Guide to Single Stock Futures.* New York: McGraw-Hill.
> Nothing has been left out. The book is, indeed, complete.

Williams, Michael S., and Amy Hoffman [2001]. *Fundamentals of the Options Market.* New York: McGraw-Hill.
> Appendix A has summary of order types. Appendix B has a summary of most option strategies. Appendix C has the various expiration cycles.

Zelkin, Marvin H. [2002]. *It's Your Option: A Trader's Primer.* Greenville, SC: Traders Press, Inc.

VOLATILITY

Brach, Marion A.[2003]. *Real Options in Practice.* New York: John Wiley & Sons.
> Different viewpoint on volatility, time decay and option pricing models such as Black-Scholes. Traders familiar with mathematical game theory and binomial decision trees will find this a must read for an alternative approach to option pricing.

Fontanills, George and Tom Gentile [2003]. *The Volatility Course.* New York: John Wiley & Sons.

McMillan, Lawrence G. [2002]. *Options as a Strategic Investment 4th Edition.* New York: New York Institute of Finance.

ONLINE BROKERS

"Active Trader's Online Brokerage Guide" [2004]. *Active Trader.* 5, 10, 28-41. (October).
> Extensive list of online brokers with considerable detail about each broker.

CHARTING SERVICES

"Traders' Resource: Data Services" [2004]. *Technical Analysis of Stocks & Commodities.* 22, 11, (November).
> Extensive list of data services.

JOURNALS LISTED ALPHABETICALLY

<u>Active Trader</u>

Active Trader Magazine
P.O. Box 567
Mt. Morris, IL 61054-0567
(800)341-9384
www.activetradermag.com
Available in most major bookstores and newsstands and by subscription.

<u>Futures</u>

P.O. Box 2122
Skokie, IL 60076-7822
(888)-804-6612
www.futures.com
Available in most bookstores and newsstands and by subscription.

<u>SFO: Stocks Futures Options</u>

Wassendorf & Associates
P.O. Box 849
Cedar Falls, IA 50613
www.sfomag.com
Available in bookstores and newsstands in financial areas and by subscription.

<u>Technical Analysis of Stocks & Commodities</u>

(800)832-4642
E-mail: circ@traders.com
www.traders.com
Available in most bookstores and newsstands and by subscription.

<u>Tradersworld</u>

Halliker's, Inc.
2508 Grayrock St.
Springfield, MO 65810
www.tradersworld.com
Available in most bookstores and newsstands and by subscription.

CHAPTER TWO

ADVANTAGES OF SWITCH STRATEGIES

The switch strategy has the following advantages over debit option spreads and straddles:
- Greater profit potential.
- Risk management is easier because the switch spread is profitable over a greater price range.
- Time decay is not a factor.
- High volatility stocks provide greater profit potential.
- Volatility skews toward the long leg have no affect on profitability.
- Under certain circumstances, an option with a low implied volatility can offer attractive profit potential.

GREATER PROFIT POTENTIAL

Option spreads involve at least one long position and at least one short position on the same underlying stock. Straddles are composed of two long (or short) positions on the same underlying stock. Some option spreads and straddles always generate a negative cash flow when opened and are called debit spreads. Other spreads and straddles always create a positive cash flow and are called credit spreads. For some spreads, such as the butterfly spread, the ideal goal is to open the spread for zero credit or debit. However, the ideal zero credit or debit situation seldom works in the heat of battle. In practice, most spreads are either credit spreads or debit spreads. It is important to distinguish between a debit spread and a margin requirement. A debit spread generates a negative cash flow. A margin requirement might be considered as collateral. The distinction is the debit spread results in cash being taken out of your account while a margin requirement does not.

The advantages of a switch credit spread over an equivalent option debit spread or straddle is illustrated using the simplest and most commonly used spread, the vertical call debit spread. The vertical call debit spread (Chapter Nine) is sometimes called a bull call spread because it is opened when the investor is slightly bullish on a particular stock. It consists of purchasing a close-to-the-money, or in-the-money, call and selling an out-of-the-money call. Both options are on the same underlying and have the same expiration date. The premium on the short out-of-the-money call is always less than the premium on the purchased, closer-to-the-money or in-of-the-money call. Therefore, the vertical call debit spread always results in a net debit.

The equivalent bull switch credit spread is constructed by switching a long single stock future for the long, lower strike call and then shorting or selling the out-of-the-money call, in that order. It is important to enter the switch trade in this order. Otherwise, until the short call position is covered by the long single stock future, the trade becomes an uncovered call with all the attendant margin requirements, minimum account balances and unlimited risk considerations of an uncovered call. The greater profit potential of the switch credit spread is illustrated using the July 29, 2003 closing prices for EBAY.

- Option Vertical Call Debit Spread
    - Buy September 105 Call   (7.60)
    - Sell September 110 Call   4.80
    - Net Debit   (2.80)
- Switch Vertical (Bull) Credit Spread
    - Buy September Single Stock Future   108.28
    - minus EBAY Close   108.14
        - Single Stock Future "Premium"   (0.14)
    - Sell September 110 call   4.80
    - Net Credit   4.66

Breakeven Points
- Option Spread
    - Lower Strike   105.00
    - plus Net Debit   2.80
        - Option Spread BEP   107.80
- Switch Spread
    - Cost of September Single Stock Future   108.28
    - minus Net Credit   4.66
    - Cost Basis of Single Stock Future and Switch Spread BEP   103.62

Maximum Gain
- Option Spread
    - Difference Between the Strikes   5.00
    - minus Net Debit   2.80
        - Option Spread Maximum Gain   2.20
- Switch Spread
    - Strike of Short Call   110.00
    - minus Cost Basis of Single Stock Future   103.62
        - Switch Spread Maximum Gain   6.38

The additional upside potential comes with a price. The option spread has a potential loss limited to the original net debit of 2.80. The switch spread has an unlimited potential loss to zero for the September single stock future. An initial protective stop loss is needed to equalize the potential loss of the two spreads. A natural initial protective stop loss price is the price where the loss from the switch spread equals the maximum loss of the option spread. The rationale is if the limited option spread loss is acceptable, then the same loss value should be acceptable for the switch spread. Assuming an initial protective stop is placed at this price, the reward/risk ratio of the switch spread is 2.28 and the reward /risk ratio of the option spread is 0.79.

Because the switch credit spread always has a lower breakeven point, the switch credit spread always has a higher profit potential. The lower breakeven point creates another advantage for the switch credit spread. In the EBAY example, the profit potential is increased by a factor of 2.9. Traders might reasonably ask, "Why not simply buy three times the number of vertical call debit spreads?" The answer to this question is based on the lower breakeven point of the switch spread.

Purchasing three EBAY bull call spreads provides approximately the same profit potential as one EBAY bull switch spread. However, the option spread breakeven point would remain the same at 105.00. This means if EBAY moved from 108.14 to 105.00 the option trade would lose 8.40 (three times the maximum loss of 2.80) while the switch spread would still be 1.38 in-the-money. This difference leads to another advantage of the switch bull call spread. If the switch bull call spread is moving against you, there is a possibility of exiting with a small profit before the spread loses money. This is not the case for the option vertical call debit spread. Unless a trader does not want to post the additional margin required for the switch trade because of the long single stock future, the option vertical call debit spread is not a very attractive alternative.

While greater potential profit is certainly a major consideration, from a risk management view-point there is a more compelling case to be made for the switch strategy. If the switch bull call spread is moving against you, there is a possibility of exiting with a small profit before the spread loses money. This is not the case for the option vertical call debit spread.

EASIER RISK MANAGEMENT

From a risk management perspective, the advantage of a switch credit spread over the equivalent option debit spread is, in most cases, the switch credit spread position starts in-the-money while the option debit spread starts out-of-the-money. In every case, the switch credit spread starts with an advantageous in-the-money position. The November 8, 2003 closing prices for NVIDIA Corporation (NVDA) illustrates this impact. A different stock is used to show that a switch spread is not materially affected by the price of the underlying. In this case, NVDA at 16.21 is used instead of EBAY at 108.14. The results are essentially the same.

- Option Vertical Call Debit Spread
    - Buy November 15.00 Call   (2.25)
    - Sell November 17.50 Call   <u>1.00</u>
        - Option Net Debit   (1.25)
- Switch Vertical (Bull) Credit Spread
    - Buy September Single Stock Future   16.23
    - NVDA Close   <u>16.21</u>
        - Single Stock Future "Premium"   (0.02)
    - Sell November 17.50 Call   <u>1.00</u>
        - Switch Net Credit   0.98

Breakeven Points
- Option Spread

Lower Strike	15.00		
plus Net Debit	1.25		
		Option Spread BEP	16.25

- Switch Spread

Cost of September Single Stock Future		16.23
minus Net Credit		0.98
Cost Basis of Single Stock Future and Switch Spread BEP		15.25

Initial In-The-Money Status
- Option Spread

Option Spread BEP	16.25	
NVDA Close	16.21	
Option Initial In-The-Money Status		(0.04)

- Switch Spread

NVDA Close	16.21	
Switch BEP	15.25	
Switch Initial In-The-Money Status		0.96

Maximum Potential Gain
- Option Spread

Difference Between the Strikes	2.50	
minus Net Debit	1.25	
Option Spread Maximum Potential Gain		1.25

- Switch Spread

Strike of Short Call	17.50	
minus Cost Basis of Single Stock Future	15.25	
Switch Spread Maximum Potential Gain		2.25

The option spread starts four cents out-of-the-money while the switch trade starts ninety-six cents in-the-money. This represents a difference of one dollar on a stock selling at 16.21. The impact of the in-the-money status can be illustrated by assuming that NVDA goes south after either position is put on. (A situation, I might say in passing, has happened to me. In fact, some days I feel my trading should be used as a contrarian indicator. Buy when I sell and sell when I buy.) In the NVDA example, the trade is never profitable and the maximum loss of 1.25 (the total debit) occurs when NVDA drops to 15.00. Since the breakeven point of the switch spread is 15.25, the switch spread will have lost 0.25 when NVDA reaches 15.00. Admittedly, both positions are in the red at 15.00. However, a 0.25 loss is five times better than a 1.25 loss. In addition, the bull switch credit spread starts in-the-money by ninety six cents which means there is a chance of exiting the trade at a small profit.

The EBAY example offers an even brighter picture. Although both positions start in-the-money, the vertical call debit spread goes negative after a decline past the BEP at 107.80. However, if EBAY goes to 105.00 the bull switch spread is still profitable by 1.38 while the option spread is experiencing its maximum loss of 2.80 (net debit). The precise initial protective stop price is a matter of the personality and the risk tolerance of the individual investor. The placement of the initial protective stop is important because a tight stop could easily be whipsawed out of existence. A suggested initial protective stop is the price where the switch spread loss equals the total net debit of the option spread. If this is considered too close, avoid the switch spread.

The lower breakeven point of the switch credit spread combined with the in-the-money start translates into more opportunities to minimize drawdown through careful position management. How the switch spread takes advantage of time decay is the next advantage that needs to be drawn out.

TIME DECAY IS NOT A FACTOR

Time is an important variable in option pricing formulas. The longer a call option has to expiration, the more time it has to increase in value. Therefore, at any given stock price, a long-term call sells for more than a short-term call. Furthermore, an option's time value decreases to zero at expiration. This is called time decay. The rate of time decay is related to the square root of the time remaining. This means that an option's time value decreases slowly at first and then time value loss rapidly accelerates as the expiration date approaches. Because of the mathematics of the curvilinear function, the rate of rapidly increasing time loss begins at about eight weeks.

The price of a single stock future is not related to the passage of time. This creates a significant advantage for switch spreads involving time such as calendar spreads (Chapter Six). Volatility can also contribute to more potential profit.

HIGH VOLATILITY STOCKS PROVIDE GREATER PROFIT POTENTIAL

This discussion assumes no volatility skew and concentrates on stocks with high volatility or options with high implied volatility. As previously pointed out, single stock future prices are not related to the volatility of the underlying stock. While volatility is not a consideration for a single stock future, volatility is a major determinant of the price of an option. Generally speaking, an option on a stock with a high volatility has a higher premium than an option on a stock with a low volatility. When there is no volatility skew, the increased premium for the long positions is usually offset by the high premium received for the short positions. When a long call is switched for a single stock future, the situation changes, high volatility works in your favor. You receive the high premium from the sale of the short call. However, because the price of the single stock future is not based on the volatility of the underlying stock, you avoid paying the high premium on the long call option portion of the spread.

How high is high volatility? Conventional wisdom says high volatility is relative and is based on an examination of historical volatility. However, only one-half of the spread derives its price based on the volatility of the underlying. Therefore, high implied volatility always works in favor of the switch spread holder because the switch trader receives the high premium from high implied volatility while the long part of the switch spread has a lower price. In summary, switch credit spreads on high volatility stocks provide greater profit potential because the high premium paid for long option positions is avoided by switching the high premium long option with a long single stock future.

VOLATILITY SKEWS TOWARD THE LONG LEG HAVE NO AFFECT ON PROFITABILITY

The prevailing view is the increased premium due to volatility has no impact on an option spread. It is felt the higher premium paid for any long calls is offset by the equally higher premium received from the sale of the short calls. A volatility skew can create a situation where this is not true. The maximum loss of a debit spread is equal to the net debit needed to open the spread. When implied volatility of the long leg(s) is significantly higher than the implied volatility of the short leg(s), the relatively higher premium paid out for the long positions is not offset by the net cash in from the sale of the relatively cheaper short positions. As a result, the amount needed to open the spread increases. When the implied volatility of the long option leg(s) of a spread is considerably higher than the implied volatility of the short leg(s) of a spread (a volatility skew), the spread in changes in four ways:

- Initial drawdown increases.
- Maximum loss (or debit) increases.
- Potential profit is less.
- The breakeven point is higher, thereby, making a potentially profitable spread unattractive because of the increased reward/risk ratio of the spread.

Initial drawdown increases because the net debit to open the spread increases. This increases the potential maximum loss of the spread because the maximum loss of a debit spread is always the amount of the initial net debit. The potential profit is less because, in most cases, the total maximum profit of a debit spread is limited to the difference between the strikes minus the net debit. For example, if the lower long strike is 70, the higher short strike is 75 and the net debit is 2.75, the maximum profit for the spread equals (75-70) – (2.75) or 2.25. When a volatility skew changes the net debit to 3.00, the maximum profit potential decreases to 2.00. The computation of maximum profit potential is slightly more complex for spreads such as butterflies and condors. However, the result is essentially the same, the higher the initial debit, the lower the maximum potential profit.

For a simple spread, such as the vertical call debit spread, the breakeven point equals the lower strike price plus the net debit. Therefore, an increase in the net debit automatically increases the breakeven point. In some instances, the breakeven point will increase to a point where the spread will become unattractive. This means the spread will not be opened even though the technical analysis setup indicates a relative high probability of success. The reason for passing up such a trading situation is obvious. The risk if you are wrong is not worth the gains if you are correct.

As pointed out before, the price of an option is determined by (1) the historical volatility of the underlying and (2) what the market thinks the volatility of the underlying will be during the life of the option. When I finally realized what this meant, I understood that there was probably a very good reason why many of the excellent technical analysis spread setups I uncovered lost money. It is because I don't have a monopoly on brains. Experienced option traders saw what I saw. They either took the other side of the trade or ignored it altogether. People who put on spreads with disadvantageous volatility skews either learn or become another statistic as a failed option trader. Sophisticated option traders are not about to make a sucker trade. Enter the switch spread.

The switch spread is ideally suited to a situation with a good technical setup and an unfavorable volatility skew. Eliminating high premiums on the long options can lower the breakeven point to a price where the reward/risk ratio becomes attractive. Of course, this will not always work. However, it will permit some potentially profitable trades that otherwise would have to be overlooked.

UNDER CERTAIN CIRCUMSTANCES, AN OPTION WITH A LOW IMPLIED VOLATILITY CAN OFFER ATTRACTIVE PROFIT POTENTIAL

The switch spread works on the idea of avoiding the high premium for a long option on a high volatility stock while receiving the premium for the short position on a high volatility stock. This logic dictates selecting stocks with high volatility as candidates for the switch spread. However, when cyclical volatility is at a low point and the trader has reason to believe a low volatility stock is about ready to breakout of a trading range and experience significantly higher volatility, a potentially profitable switch trade might be uncovered.

Historical volatility tends to move in cycles with clear turning points at the top and bottom of each cycle. When the volatility of the stock is at the extreme low point of the cycle, it is reasonable to expect an increase in volatility. The increased volatility will result in a price movement either up or down. The direction of the price movement cannot be predicted by an analysis of volatility. A long at-the-money straddle (Chapter Eight) is often used in this situation. The long straddle becomes a candidate for a switch trade when the single stock future is close to a strike price. When this happens, switching a long single stock future for the long call results in a lower net debit for the switch straddle. The net debit of the switch straddle is decreased by the amount of the premium for the long call. Therefore, a switch straddle with the long single stock future can significantly change the breakeven point and potential profit picture of a straddle.

A stock with low volatility combined with a single stock future selling below the price of the underlying also offers attractive vertical spread possibilities. When this happens, the switch spread generates a credit on the short position plus a credit on the long position. The credit on the short option position is equal to the income from the sale of the short option. When added to the credit received from the short options, the credit resulting from the discounted price of the long single stock future can lower the breakeven point to a price that makes the switch spread attractive while the option debit spread is not viable.

CONCLUSION

Switch spreads and straddles create trading opportunities that would not be appropriate using traditional spread techniques. These advantages are:

- Greater profit potential.
- Risk management is easier because the switch spread is profitable over a greater price range.
- Time decay is not a factor.
- High volatility stocks provide greater profit potential.
- Volatility skews toward the long leg have no affect on profitability.
- Under certain circumstances, an option with a low implied volatility can offer attractive profit potential.

These advantages are best realized using the selection criteria discussed in the next chapter.

REFERENCES

Crask, Mitch [2004]. *Reply to Margin Question [Crask 2003] In Your Letters. Stocks, Futures, Options*, 3, 2 (February), p.12.
> First use of the term switch spread. Explains the difference between a margin requirement and net debit for a debit spread.

Crask, Mitch [2003]. *Single Stock Futures Add a New Twist to Options Play. Stocks, Futures, Options,* 2, 11 (November), pp. 42-46.

Fontanills, George and Tom Gentile [2003]. *The Volatility Course.* New York: John Wiley & Sons.

McMillan, Lawrence G. [2002]. *Options as a Strategic Investment 4th Edition.* New York: New York Institute of Finance.

Wasendorf, Russell [2004]. *The Complete Guide to Single Stock Futures.* New York: McGraw-Hill.

CHAPTER THREE

SCREENING CRITERIA

BASIC STRATEGY

The basic strategy is fourfold:

- Lower position breakeven points by turning option debit positions into equivalent switch credit positions,
- use both historical and implied volatility as a tool to increase position profitability,
- create positions that take advantage of the time decay of options and
- have a plan to manage the affects of downside risk.

This chapter presents screening criteria designed to accomplish the first three strategies. Position and risk management considerations are discussed in Chapter Five. Position, dependent position and risk management considerations are discussed in the chapters covering each switch spread.

SCREENING CRITERIA FOR SWITCH STRATEGY CANDIDATES

The screening criteria for switch spreads are:

1. Limit the use of the switch strategy to debit spreads and straddles where the short positions are calls.
2. As a general statement, select an underlying with a market price that has a favorable relationship to the strike prices of the switch spread or straddle being placed. Although this sounds like a motherhood and apple pie statement, it is not. For example a switch straddle should have the underlying price close to the strike while for a vertical call debit spread the underlying price should be above the midway point between two adjacent strikes.
3. Use options and single stock futures on stocks with volatility at the extremes (high or low) in their volatility cycle.
4. Use spreads and straddles whose options have a high implied volatility compared to the volatility of the underlying.
5. Construct the short leg(s) of the spread with options that have between six and ten weeks to expiration.
6. The single stock future must be at, or close to, fair market value.

LIMIT USE TO STRADDLES AND DEBIT SPREADS
WHERE THE SHORT POSITIONS ARE CALLS

Although the profit potential of some credit spreads can be enhanced by a switch spread, the increased margin and risk are usually not worth substituting a switch spread for a credit option spread. Short puts are excluded because of the inability to provide a switch spread with a covered put in the same sense of switch spread with a covered call. The two exceptions are the iron butterfly (Chapter Twelve) and the box spread discussed in Chapter Thirteen. A debit straddle consists of the purchase of a call option and the simultaneous purchase of a put on the same stock with the same strike and the same expiration date. A spread consists of purchased options and written options on the same underlying stock. The options bought and sold will have different strike prices or different expiration months, or they may have both different strikes and different expiration months. A stock option spread is an investment strategy that uses two options with the goal of limiting risk and increasing the probability of profit. The goal of a spread is to have one leg of the spread make enough profit to cover the unprofitable leg(s) of the spread with something left over for profit. Sometimes, but not often, it is possible to make a profit on more than one leg of a spread. Conditions creating this possibility are discussed under the Position Management section of the appropriate strategies. The process of buying and selling the options constituting a spread is called *putting on* or *placing* the spread. When you *take off* or *lift* or *close* a spread you buy and sell in reverse order. The term *offsetting* is the term most often used for taking off or closing a single stock future position.

SELECT AN UNDERLYING WITH A MARKET PRICE THAT HAS A FAVORABLE
RELATIONSHIP TO THE STRIKE PRICES OF THE SWITCH SPREAD

When the strike price is far above the stock price, the premium is relatively low and the volatility and time factors have little impact. This is important for two reasons:

- The closer the stock price is to the strike price of the short option, the higher the price of the short option. This means a higher credit from the sale of the short option.
- The time value premium is greatest when the stock price and the striking price are the same. Therefore, using this criteria increases the option price of the short option by increasing the time value component of the option price.

This criterion is illustrated using EBAY, NVDA and ALTR. Complete data for EBAY and NVDA are provided in Chapter Two. The maximum gain information for EBAY and NVDA are repeated below.

Maximum Limited Potential Gain for EBAY
- Option Spread
  - Difference Between the Strikes   5.00
  - minus Net Debit   2.80
    - EBAY Option Spread Maximum Gain   2.20
- Switch Spread
  - Strike of Short Call   110.00
  - minus Single Stock Future Cost Basis   103.62
    - EBAY Switch Spread Maximum Gain   6.38

Maximum Limited Potential Gain for NVDA.
- Option Spread

Difference Between the Strikes	2.50	
minus Net Debit	1.25	
NVDA Option Spread Maximum Gain		1.25

- Switch Spread

Strike of Short Call	17.50	
minus Single Stock Future Cost Basis	15.25	
NVDA Switch Spread Maximum Gain		2.25

Relevant ALTR data are provided below.
- Option Vertical Call Debit Spread

Buy November 17.50 Call	(1.79)	
Sell November 20 Call	0.70	
ALTR Option Spread Net Debit		(1.09)

- Switch Vertical (Bull) Credit Spread

Buy November Single Stock Future	18.09	
ALTR Close	17.99	
November Single Stock Future "Premium"	(0.10)	
Sell November 20 call	0.70	
ALTR Switch Spread Net Credit		0.60

Breakeven Points
- Option Spread

Lower Strike	17.50	
plus Net Debit	1.09	
ALTR Option Spread BEP		18.59

- Switch Spread

November Single Stock Future Cost	18.09	
minus Net Credit	0.60	
Single Stock Future Cost Basis and ALTR Switch Spread BEP		17.49

Maximum Limited Potential Gain
- Option Spread

Difference Between the Strikes	2.50	
minus Net Debit	1.09	
ALTR Option Spread Maximum Gain		1.41

- Switch Spread

Strike of Sold Call	20.00	
minus Single Stock Future Cost Basis	17.49	
ALTR Switch Spread Maximum Gain		2.51

Figure 3.1: Gain Ratio Comparisons For A Switch Spread vs. An Option Spread

Symbol	Last As Percentage Of Difference Between The Strikes	Type Of Spread	Max Gain	Switch/Option Max Gain Ratio
ALTR	19.6%	option spread	1.50	1.74
		switch spread	2.61	
NVDA	48.4%	option spread	1.25	1.80
		switch spread	2.25	
EBAY	62.8%	option spread	2.20	2.90
		switch spread	6.38	

Figure 3.1 provides a comparison of the maximum potential gain for both the switch spread and the option spread in terms of the underlying stock price as a percentage of the difference between the strikes.

When the last as a percentage of the difference between the strikes increases, so does the maximum gain ratio for the switch spread. However, this is not a straight line relationship. Research indicates a curvilinear function similar to an "S" curve. Research also indicates that the point at which the curve begins to accelerate is near the fifty percent value. For the vertical call debit spread, the closer the stock price is to the upper strike, the greater the relative gain for the switch spread. However, the absolute value of the maximum potential gain is independent of the ratio of the gain between the option and switch spreads. For example, the maximum gain ratio is 1.80 for NVDA and 1.78 for ALTR. However, the maximum gain in dollars is less for NVDA than for ALTR. The reason for this is the mathematical impact (or lack thereof) of volatility and time decay on the price of an out-of-the-money option.

When the switch spread does not offer a significant relative advantage, the trader should consider using the traditional option spread. Of course, what constitutes a significant advantage depends on each investor's personality and definition of risk. The higher the volatility the less impact this criterion has on the switch spread. This leads to a consideration of the next criteria for the switch spread, *i.e.*, volatility.

USE OPTIONS AND SINGLE STOCK FUTURES ON STOCKS WITH VOLATILITY AT THE EXTREMES (HIGH OR LOW) IN THEIR VOLATILITY CYCLE

Call option sellers demand more money for a stock that has the ability to move a relatively large distance upward. The additional premium is needed to offset the higher risk of being exercised. Likewise, buyers will be willing to pay more for the option because there is a greater chance of the option becoming profitable. Therefore, an option on a stock with a high volatility has a higher premium than an option on a stock with a low volatility. The prevailing view is that the increased premium due to volatility has no impact on debit spreads. It is felt the higher premium paid for the long call is offset by the higher premium received from the sale of the short call.

When the long option is replaced by a long single stock future the situation changes. You still receive the high premium for the sale of the short call. However, because the price of the single stock future is not based on the volatility of the underlying stock, the high premium on the long call option portion of the spread is avoided. This results in four advantages for the switch strategy:

- Debit spreads composed of options with high implied volatilities become credit spreads.
- A debit spread with a volatility skew toward the long options can present an opportunity that is not present with traditional spreads.
- A debit spread with a low implied volatility for both short and long options may become a viable alternative that can capitalize on anticipated increased volatility of the underlying stock.
- When the short options with high implied volatility change to low implied volatility options, otherwise losing positions can sometimes be exited at a small profit.

USE SPREADS AND STRADDLES WHOSE OPTIONS HAVE A HIGH IMPLIED VOLATILITY COMPARED TO THE VOLATILITY OF THE UNDERLYING

The switch spread or straddle is particularly useful when option prices reflect a higher implied volatility than the historical volatility of the underlying stock. This situation does not prevent opening an option spread because the extra premium paid for the long legs is offset by the extra premium received from the sale of the short legs. However, when a single stock future is switched for the purchased options, the potential gain is increased and the break even point is lowered. The greater potential of the switch credit spread is illustrated using the July 29, 2003 closing prices for EBAY from Chapter Two.

```
Option Vertical Call Debit Spread
        Buy September 105 Call            (7.60)
        Sell September 110 Call            4.80
                            Net Debit         (2.80)
Switch Vertical (Bull) Credit Spread
    Buy September Single Stock Future    108.28
    EBAY Close                           108.14
        Single Stock Future "Premium"         (0.14)
        Sell September 110 call                4.80
                            Net Credit        4.66
```

Volatilities

EBAY	0.260
September 105 Call	0.350
September 110 Call	0.333

The price of the September 105 call option is 7.60. This is 1.29 more than the theoretical price of 6.31 based on the volatility of EBAY. The price of the September 110 call is 4.80 which is 1.08 more than the theoretical price. This appears to be a relatively close fit to the theory that the high cost paid for the long option is offset by the high amount received for the short option. However, by switching a September single stock future for the long September 105 call, the debit for the long position is reduced from 7.60 (the price of the September 105 call) to 0.14 (the September single stock future "Premium"). This increases the maximum gain from 2.20 to 6.38. It also decreases the breakeven point from 107.80 to 103.61. The calculations are given below.

EBAY Maximum Potential Gain
- Option Spread

Difference Between the Strikes	5.00	
minus Net Debit	2.80	
Option Spread Maximum Potential Gain		2.20

- Switch Spread

Strike of Short Call	110.00	
minus Cost Basis of Single Stock Future	103.62	
Switch Spread Maximum Potential Gain		6.38

EBAY Breakeven Points
- Option Spread

Lower Strike	105.00	
plus Net Debit	2.80	
Option Spread BEP		107.80

- Switch Spread

Cost of September single stock future	108.28	
minus Net Credit	4.66	
Switch Spread BEP		103.62

This works because the high cost of the purchased call is avoided by switching a single stock future for the long position.

CONSTRUCT THE SHORT LEG(S) OF THE SPREAD WITH OPTIONS THAT HAVE BETWEEN SIX AND TEN WEEKS TO EXPIRATION

Make time decay work in your favor. The longer a call option has to expiration, the more time it has to increase in value. Therefore, at any given stock price, a long-term call sells for more than a short-term call. Furthermore, an option's time value decreases to zero at expiration. This is called time decay. The rate of time decay is related to the square root of the time remaining. This means an option's time value decreases slowly at first and then time value loss rapidly accelerates as the expiration date approaches. Because of the mathematics of the curvilinear function, the rate of rapidly increasing time loss begins at about eight weeks.

Choosing an expiration date greater than six weeks permits capturing some of the time premium when the close-to-the-money option is sold. Limiting the time to expiration to ten weeks permits taking advantage of time decay. This works because a single stock future does not experience time decay.

SINGLE STOCK FUTURE MUST BE AT FAIR MARKET VALUE

When a single stock future is not at, or near, the fair market value, either wait for arbitrage to correct the situation or check the assumptions about either the interest rate or the dividends. When arbitrage does not correct the situation, there is something amiss. Avoid the trade.

CONCLUSION

This chapter presents the six criteria for identifying switch spread candidates. They are:

1. Limit the use of the switch strategy to debit spreads and straddles where the short positions are calls.
2. As a general statement, select an underlying with a market price that has a favorable relationship to the strike prices of the switch spread or straddle being placed. Although this sounds like a motherhood and apple pie statement it is not. For example a switch straddle should have the underlying price close to the strike while for a vertical call debit spread the underlying price should be above the midway point between two adjacent strikes.
3. Use options and single stock futures on stocks with volatility at the extremes (high or low) in their volatility cycle.
4. Use spreads and straddles whose options have a high implied volatility compared to the volatility of the underlying.
5. Construct the short leg(s) of the spread with options that have between six and ten weeks to expiration.
6. The single stock future must be at, or close to, fair market value.

All switch spreads generated using these criteria offer greater profit potential and lower breakeven points. The downside is the increased margin requirements and the potentially unlimited risk of the single stock futures component. The potentially unlimited risk must be properly managed (See Chapter Five and Chapter Six.)

REFERENCES

Crask, Mitch [2003]. *Single Stock Futures Add a New Twist to Options Play. Stocks, Futures, Options,* 2, 11 (November), pp. 42-46.

Fontanills, George and Tom Gentile [2003]. *The Volatility Course.* New York: John Wiley & Sons.

McMillan, Lawrence G. [2002]. *Options as a Strategic Investment. 4th Edition.* New York: New York Institute of Finance.

Wasendorf, Russell [2004]. *The Complete Guide to Single Stock Futures.* New York: McGraw-Hill.

CHAPTER FOUR

TECHNICAL ANALYSIS REVIEW

BASIS OF TECHNICAL ANALYSIS

This is not a book on technical analysis. However, a brief overview of some of the technical analysis used for switch spreads is needed to provide a background for the rest of the book. Useful references on support and resistance, technical chart patterns, candlestick analysis, Fibonacci analysis, Elliott Wave analysis and point and figure charts are found at the end of this chapter.

The basis of technical trading is price. First, when prices for any particular day are dramatically below the previous day's prices, investors consider selling if they believe the price differential represents the beginning of a reversal from an uptrend to a significant downtrend. A major contributing factor for a sell-off is the price differential between two or more days. Secondly, daily, weekly, and monthly price patterns help identify trends, reversal points and the sideways movements that are essential to receiving the maximum return on your investment. Thirdly, price normally reflects all available information. Investors with special knowledge about an impending event normally buy and sell until the current price reflects their evaluation of the impact of the information. Therefore, when the news is released, the impact of the information is already reflected in the price. This idea is summarized in the stock market rule: ***"Buy on the rumor — Sell on the news."***

Technical analysis also provides representations of the psychology of financial markets. It measures the emotions and actions of the investment community. Technical analysis represents how investors are reacting as the market is going against them. — FEAR. Technical analysis illustrates how investors are reacting when they believe they might be missing a major market move.— GREED. Technical analysis shows what investors are doing as they attempt to squeeze the last few pennies out of an uptrend. — GREED. Technical analysis demonstrates the extent of investor confusion as they watch a market move sideways. — INDECISION.

I am often asked where a good technical analysis chart provider can be found. One good source is "Traders' Resource: Data Services" [2004]. *Technical Analysis of Stocks & Commodities*. 22, 11, (November). Some commonly used journals that cover technical analysis are listed in the references section of this chapter.

A brief review of resistance, support and gap analysis is provided. Traders familiar with these ideas may want to skip these sections. However, experienced trades may want to check the sections on candlesticks and Fibonacci analysis. The candlestick section provides two twists on candlestick analysis I have found useful for option spreads. The Fibonacci section provides an application of Fibonacci analysis I have not seen in discussions of Fibonacci analysis applied to the stock market.

RESISTANCE AND SUPPORT

RESISTANCE ~ Stocks have a price level above which they do not seem to want to trade. Stocks will go up to this price and then either stay there or go back down. This upper price level is called the resistance price.

Usually, when a stock price hits a resistance price level, the resistance price level is stretched, or tested, and the stock goes back down again. This temporary excursion above the resistance price level is called a "test of the resistance price level." Sometimes the resistance price level is stretched like a rubber band but it does not break. When this happens, the price usually reacts by dropping quite rapidly. Occasionally, a stock hits a resistance level and stays near the resistance level for a period of time. In this case the stock is said to be testing the resistance level. Finally the stock takes a breather, trades sideways, and then continues the uptrend. When a stock breaks a resistance price level and breaks out in an uptrend, it often reaches a new peak or resistance level, and then quickly retreats to the old resistance level which then becomes a support level.

SUPPORT ~ Stocks have a price level, or floor, below which they do not seem to want to trade. When a support price level is reached, one of two things happens: either the stock price goes back up or the stock takes a breather, trades sideways, and then continues down. When a stock does not pause at a support price level, the stock could be headed for trouble. Support price levels are drawn by connecting the troughs on a stock chart. A support level depends on the time period used. Most stocks have more than one support level over a twelve-month time period. In practice, the longer a support price has been in effect, the more significant it becomes. Normally when the price of a stock breaks one support level it falls until it hits the next lower, fallback support level or, alternatively, when the price of a stock breaks one resistance level it rises until it hits the next higher resistance level. Normally, after an uptrend, a stock tries to find a new support level at a higher price level. When a new support level does not hold, the stock usually retreats to a lower, longer-term support level.

To oversimplify:
- Resistance price levels become support price levels.
- Support price levels become resistance price levels.
- Support price levels on the way up become support price levels on the way down and resistance levels on the way down become resistance levels on the way up.

The point in a downtrend where support becomes resistance is called crossover support to resistance. The point in an uptrend where resistance becomes support is called crossover resistance to support.

CROSSOVER RESISTANCE TO SUPPORT ~ Figure 4.1 shows an extended uptrend and downtrend by Conseco, Inc. (CNC). Resistance is indicated by an **R**, support is indicated by an **S**, crossover resistance to support is indicated by **R/S**, and crossover support to resistance is represented by **S/R**. Notice there are five support price levels going up. How can there be more than one support price level? A stock almost never goes straight up. A stock in an uptrend usually has consolidation plateaus where the stock takes a breather and gets ready for the next stage of the uptrend. The entire graph can be viewed as a multi-story building with each support level representing the floor of each story. Figure 4.1 can be viewed as a five-story building. Once a person has gone from floor one to floor two, it takes more effort to go back down to floor one or go up to floor three than to stay on floor two. The same is true of a stock price.

The point is support levels on the way up become potential support levels on the way down. On the way up support price levels were established at 20, 30, 40, 50, and 60. Except for support at 60, these support levels were repeated on the way down. Somebody out there will notice that this is not exactly correct. Figure 4.1 uses a support price level of 32 rather than 30. However, we are not talking rocket science. Remember, support price levels on the way down are estimates. The amount of precision needed is a function of the data available and the amount of risk an investor is willing to take.

FIGURE 4.1: CROSSOVER RESISTANCE TO SUPPORT AND VICE VERSA

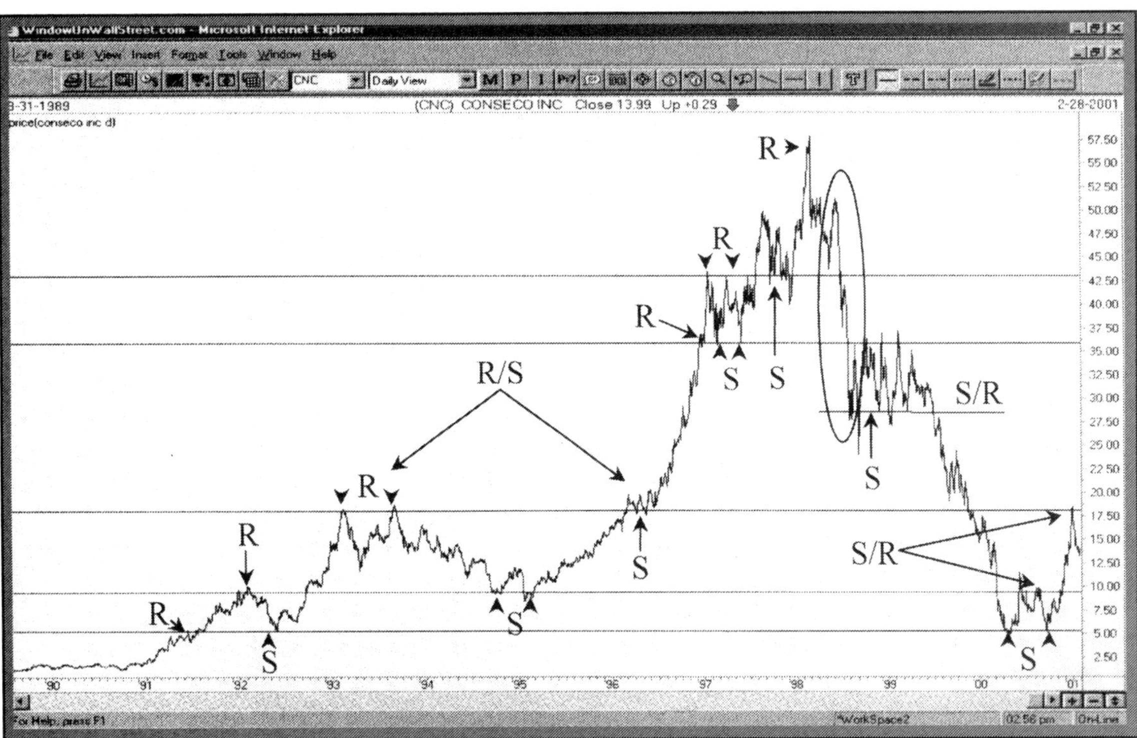

Sometimes, a stock is sold too soon. Profits are lost when the stock recovers. However, holding a stock that is going down in the hope of recovering losses is a profitable strategy only for experienced investors. Of course, the best way to become an experienced investor is to lose money by holding stocks that are going down in the hope that they will recover and become profitable. Experienced investors call this "Hold and Hope."

Except for the last support price level on the way up, Conseco tends to pause on the way down near prices where it paused on the way up. The fact that Conseco does not pause at the top support level is the first indication that Conseco might be reversing direction from an uptrend to a downtrend. The second indication that Conseco is headed south is that it goes into free fall through the next support level and stops at a temporary support level of 28.00. When a stock falls through multiple support levels, it becomes a falling knife. A commonly quoted stock market rule is: ***"Never try to catch a falling knife."***

GAPS

When the high on one day is below the low of the previous day, a gap in trading prices occurs. For these two days, there was a price range in which the stock did not trade. This space on a chart is called a gap. There are four types of gaps:
- a common gap (C),
- a breakaway gap (B),
- a measurement or continuation gap (M) and
- an exhaustion gap (E).

FIGURE 4.2: GAP ANALYSIS

FIGURE 4.2 (page 32) is a weekly chart for Hewlett Packard Co. (HPQ) showing examples of all four gaps. A common gap is quickly filled and is usually smaller than the other three gaps. It is often found in sideways markets. A breakaway gap down occurs after an extended uptrend has begun to turn downward and signals a possible trend reversal or retracement. The expectation is the stock is beginning a downtrend. The breakaway gap is confirmed if the gap is not closed after a short period of time. The top, midpoint and bottom of the gap become resistance levels. A measurement or continuation down gap forms after a downtrend has been in progress for some time. It is called a continuation gap because, if it is not filled, it signals a continuation of the downtrend. If confirmed, a target for the end of the downtrend can be calculated by subtracting the price at the gap from the beginning of the downtrend. When this value is subtracted from the price at the gap the result provides a value for the end of the downtrend. An exhaustion gap indicates the last flurry of selling. It is important to realize that an exhaustion gap does not signal a reversal from a downtrend to an uptrend. It simply indicates the downtrend is probably over. After an exhaustion gap, stocks often trade sideways over an extended period of consolidation.

The candlestick version of any gap is called a trading window. The idea is, as long as trading windows are not closed, the current uptrend or downtrend will continue (See Chapter One, Nison [2001]).

CANDLESTICK ANALYSIS

Knowledge of candlestick analysis is assumed. Those without this knowledge can find the basic references at the end of this chapter. The role of long white candlesticks to establish support, confirm support and signal when support is broken and a similar use of long black candlesticks for resistance is pointed out in Chapter One of *Beyond Candlesticks* by Steve Nison [1994]. The success of an option spread is considerably enhanced when this technique is included in the setup for the trade.

For long white bodies, the technique works like this. Three lines are drawn: one line from the open at the bottom, a second line from the close at the top and a third line from the midpoint between the open and the close. These lines represent potential support areas. **FIGURE 4.3** (page 34) gives a daily chart of Amazon.com, Inc., (AMZN) that shows how this works with long white bodies in an uptrend.

FIGURE 4.3: LONG WHITE BODIES AS SUPPORT

Four long white bodies form support levels for the uptrend. The long white body at **A** represents the beginning of the uptrend. The open and close are represented by two solid black lines. The midpoint is represented by the dotted line between the two solid black lines. AMZN goes slightly above the long white body at **A** and then retreats to the dotted line at the midpoint. Two bars have shadows that approach the opening line. However, only one bar closes below the doted line at the midpoint. This means the dotted line for bar **A** represents a support level. When AMZN breaks the top solid line of bar **A**, a continuation of the uptrend can be expected. This uptrend continues for one month and then retreats to retest support at bar **A**. Support at the closing line of bar **A** holds during the week of July 21, 2003. Fibonacci and Elliott Wave analysts will recognize this pattern as a five wave pattern with a retracement that could be forming the first wave of a larger trend. The lines drawn based on bar A provide guidelines for a support area from which an uptrend could be forming. A trader who wished to micro analyze the chart could include the black body and white black body between **A** and **B**. This usually clutters the chart rather than helps analysis. From an option trading viewpoint, bar **A** gives a high probability set up for an upward move of the underlying which resulted in a short-term bullish move through three strike prices (35.00, 37.50 and 40.00) in two weeks. During this move an up gap long white body formed at **B**. The midpoint of this bar also formed a new support level and another bullish option set up. After forming a new support level at the midpoint of bar **B** and after

34

clearly breaking the upper closing bar line of bar **B** with another long white body, AMZN moved from a price near the 42.50 strike through three strikes (45.00, 47.50 and 50.00) in six weeks. Fibonacci and Elliott Wave analysts will recognize this as a large wave three containing five smaller waves. However, using the long-white-bodies-form-support approach results in option trades that capture most of the move without using the more complex analyses. The long white bar at **D** provides another trading setup. When the upper line of **D** is clearly broken, AMZN goes from halfway between strikes at 50 and 55 through the 55 strike and closes near the 60 strike within three weeks.

Viewing long white bodies as potential support areas provides convenient protective stop points when a single stock future is switched for one of the option positions in a spread or straddle. With a debit spread, the maximum loss is always known when the spread is opened. The maximum loss is always equal to the net debit. This is not the case for switch spreads. Using long white bodies to generate support areas provides rational places for protective stops to guard against any potential unlimited loss from the single stock future portion of the switch spread. Long white body support areas also provide rational targets for price movements during retracements. As long as you don't overkill and draw lines from every long white body, this strategy can be uncanny in its accuracy. Long black bodies are not discussed but the same principles apply in reverse.

FIGURE 4.4: RICKSHAW MEN

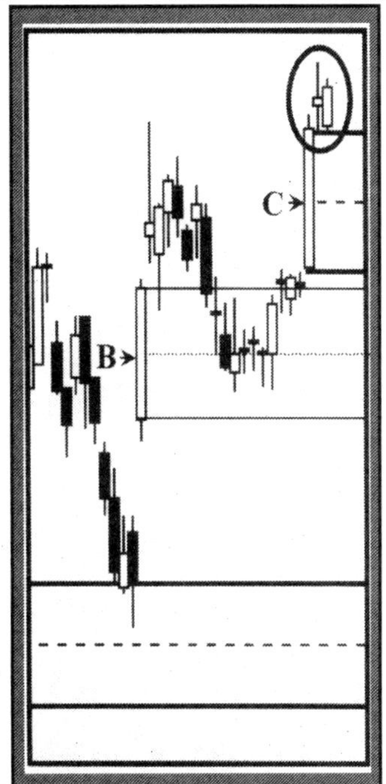

In addition to the use of long bodies as support and resistance, there is one twist on traditional candlestick analysis that I have found useful for option spreads. It is a modification of the rickshaw man and is shown in **FIGURE 4.4** which is a blowup of the Bar **C** area in Figure 4.3. Doji and spinning tops at the end of uptrends and downtrends are used as reversal signals. However, when they occur in the middle of a trend or in a sideways market they are said to provide no trading signals. They are called rickshaw men because they are said to be carrying the trend or sideways movement along.

After studying Nison's second book on candlesticks, *Beyond Candlesticks,* I noticed trend continuation signals are often generated when spinning tops and Doji were coupled with long white (or long black) bodies. I reserved the name "Rickshaw Men" to refer to such a situation because the spinning tops are truly "transporting the trend along." The circled bars in Figure 4.4 are two such bars.

The trading criteria are:
- The pattern must occur in a well established uptrend or downtrend. It is not useful for stocks trading sideways.
- The close of the spinning tops should remain close to or above the top, or close, of the long white body.
- The low of the spinning tops should not penetrate the midpoint of the long white body.
- More than three spinning tops cancel the pattern.
- The appearance of Doji weakens the signal.
- Look for an uptrend continuation when the **A** bar closes above the highest high (lowest low for a downtrend) of the spinning top rickshaw men.

Figure 4.4 is also a modification of a candlestick pattern called a rising window discussed in Chapter Seven of *Japanese Candlestick Charting Techniques* by Nison [2001]. A thorough statistical test of the rickshaw man pattern has not been completed. It is offered because it has proven useful for placing trailing protective stops and for reentering an uptrend. The same pattern using black bodies holds for downtrends.

FIBONACCI ANALYSIS

See the references at the end of this chapter for several excellent books on Fibonacci analysis. One application of Fibonacci analysis I have not seen in discussions of Fibonacci analysis applied to the stock market is the Fibonacci implications of reflections of a ray of light through panes of glass. This is not as far out at it seems.

The idea is that when a ray of light encounters a pane of glass it can either be reflected back by the outer surface, pass directly through with no reflection, or enter the pane of glass and be reflected back by the edge opposite the edge through which it entered. **FIGURE 4.5** presents some of the reflection paths that have obvious parallels in technical analysis. When two panes of glass, P1 and P2, are placed together, three reflective surfaces are created: the outer edge facing the light source (E1), the interface between the two panes of glass (I), and the outer edge opposite the light source (E2). Some obvious similarities to technical analysis patterns are shown in Figure 4.5.

FIGURE 4.5: DIFFERENT LIGHT RAY PATHS THROUGH TWO PANES OF GLASS

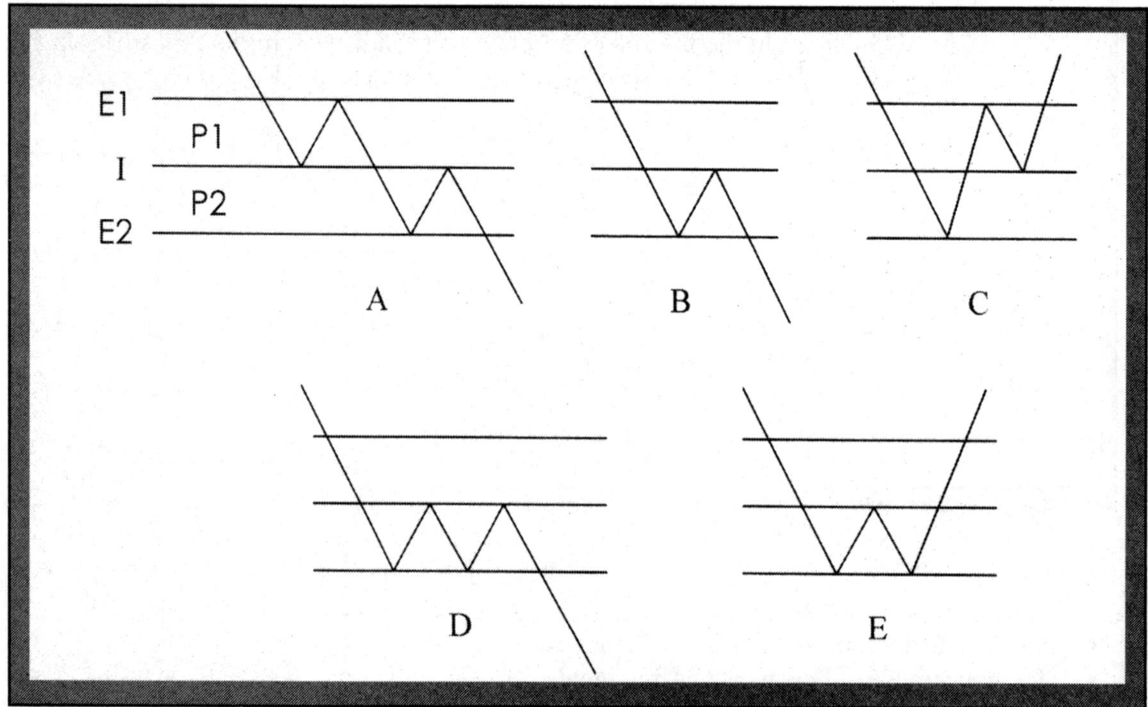

Reflection path **A** represents a five-wave Elliott Impulse Wave. Reflection path **B** represents a fifty percent Dow or Fibonacci retracement before continuing a downtrend. Reflection path **C** represents a **"V"** bottom. Reflection path **D** could represent either an Elliott Wave zigzag wave 2 or it could represent the failure of a third test of support. Reflection path **E** represents a **"W"** bottom.

Additional dimensions are added to the analysis when more panes of glass are considered and when the light is allowed to travel along the interfaces between the two panes. For example, Fibonacci pivot points appear to become more robust when viewed as interfaces between multiple panes of glass with different thickness. Also included in the references provided is a new way to draw Fibonacci time intervals using the golden rectangle.

The mathematics of the process is recommended for those with a mathematical background. For those with no mathematical background, take heart. I discovered the idea on a web page designed for grade school students. It is not necessary to understand the mathematics to use the idea. For example, a spear fisherman does not have to understand the mathematics of the refraction of light by water to become an excellent fisherman.

POINT AND FIGURE ANALYSIS

Point and figure analysis is not covered here. For an excellent discussion of point and figure charting see the Second Edition of *Point & Figure Charting* by Thomas J. Dorsey. Point and figure charts have been around for over 100 years. Because they use only one dimension, price, they are easy to understand, volume and time are not considerations. This is an important point for the long-term investor who is more interested in IF rather than WHEN a security is going to recover. The following reading order is recommended: pp. 19-34; pp. 34-44; pp. 207-225; pp. 236-240; Chapter Nine with particular attention to the six rules for stock selection beginning on page 248. Finally, skim pp. 51-83 and the rest of the book. Return to pp. 51-83 for reference purposes as needed. This proven method of tracking fluctuations between the supply and demand for securities allows the investor to recognize promising or dangerous trends early enough to take advantage of them.

COMBINING TECHNICAL INDICATORS TO INCREASE GAINS

The seven main areas of technical analysis are:
- Support and Resistance.
- Technical Patterns Such as Triangles and "W" Bottoms.
- Candlestick Analysis.
- Gap Analysis also Called Windows in Candlestick Analysis.
- Fibonacci Analysis Which is Often Combined With Elliott Wave Analysis.
- Elliott Wave Analysis Which is Often Combined With Fibonacci Analysis.
- Point and Figure Charts.

There is no silver bullet in technical analysis. The best that can be done is increase the probability of being correct by combining several methods. If several methods, with no correlation between them, give the same signal, the probability of being correct increases. For statistical studies with historical probabilities for technical patterns such as ascending triangles and "W" bottoms see *Ency-*

clopedia of Chart Patterns by Bulkowski [2000]. For a thorough statistical study of the probabilities and timing of candlestick patterns see *Candlestick Charting Explained* by Morris [1992]. Some traders with a quantitative bent use subjective probabilities and decision trees. Personally, I don't find the added information provided by Bayesian subjective probabilities and decision tree analysis worth the effort. However, there are many who would disagree with this statement. **FIGURE 4.6** provides an example of how resistance and support, technical patterns, candlestick analysis, and gap analysis can be combined to identify a reversal pattern.

Notice how the long white bodies (A, B, C, D) provide support areas on the way up, as well as, support on the way down. The advance block candlestick pattern (1) indicates a potential end to the uptrend. The exhaustion gap (2) provides another signal the uptrend is probably ending. Finally, the ascending triangle (3) ending in a shooting star (4) is followed by a down gap which forms a pattern called an island top (3) with a dead cat bounce (5). The Dead Cat Bounce is an easy formation to spot. There is a large down gap followed by an apparent recovery or bounce. People owning the stock are wondering if they should sell. People who do not own the stock are wondering if it is a bargain. An experienced investor would say: If you own it, sell it...If you don't own it, don't buy it! The dead cat bounce is one of the few technical patterns that can be directly linked to fundamental analysis. It usually indicates an, as yet unknown, fundamental weakness. The top of the bounce represents a strong resistance area which, if broken, indicates a false signal and a continuation of the uptrend. However, when the top of the bounce is not broken an extended sideways or downtrend lasting at least one year is indicated.

FIGURE 4.3: LONG WHITE BODIES AS SUPPORT

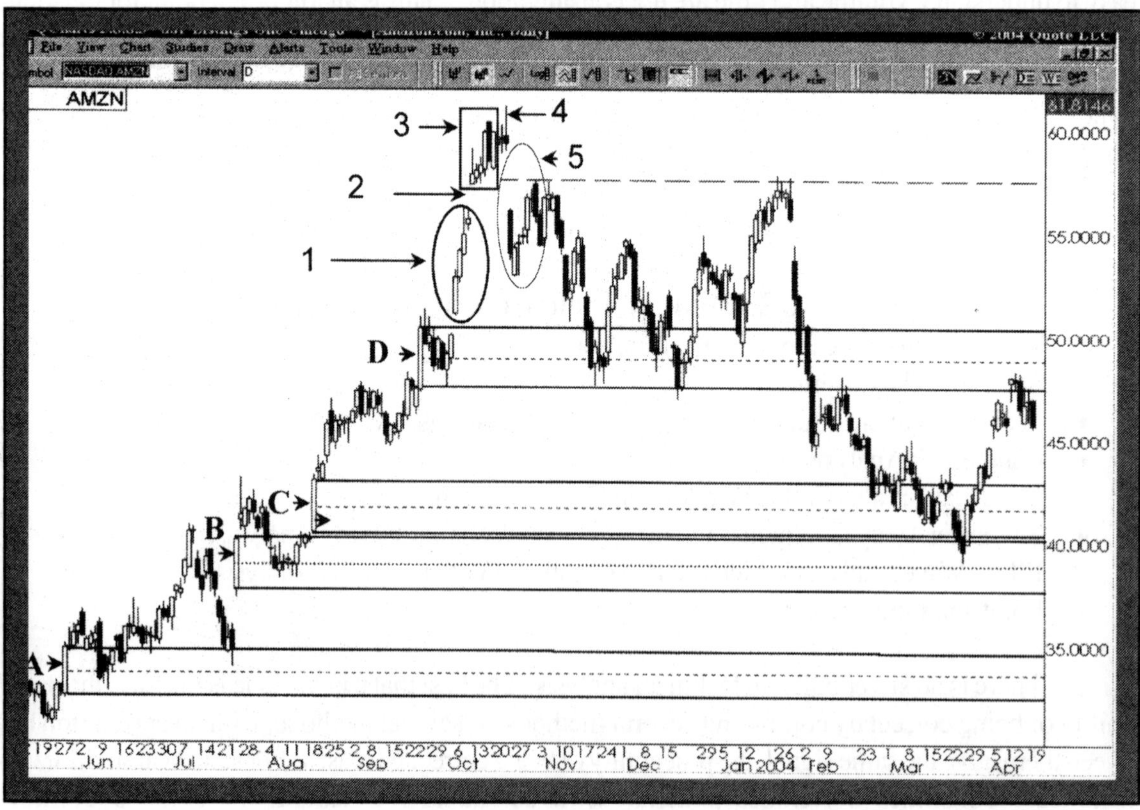

Figure 4.6 does not include an Elliott Wave count (Frost and Prechter [1999]) or Fibonacci pivot points (Hobbs [2003]). However, experienced Elliott Wave traders will recognize the reversal signals appearing at the end of a complex five-wave uptrend. Elliott Wave analysts will also recognize the obvious A, B, C patterns which form at the end of a major uptrend or downtrend. Fibonacci lines would clutter the chart beyond recognition. However, Fibonacci ratios and pivot points also confirm a reversal of the uptrend (Hobbs [2003]).

When this many different types of reversal signals indicate an end to an uptrend, you don't have to be clairvoyant to know the uptrend is probably coming to an end.

CONCLUSION

A brief overview is provided for

- resistance,
- support,
- crossover resistance to support and crossover support to resistance,
- and gap analysis.

Two candlestick applications are provided that have proven useful for option spread trading. They are:

- the use of long white and long black bodies as support and resistance levels and
- a new way to look at rickshaw men.

Finally, a potential new application of Fibonacci analysis is presented which is based on research from non-financial areas. The work is based on the implications of reflections of a ray of light through panes of glass.

REFERENCES

Bigalow, Steve [2004]. *Market Timing with Candlesticks. Technical Analysis of Stocks and Commodities, 22*, 5, pp. 88-90.

Bigalow, Steven W. [2002]. *Profitable Candlestick Trading.* New York: John Wiley & Sons.

Bollinger, John [2002]. *Bollinger on Bollinger Bands.* New York: McGraw-Hill.

Brown, Constance [2002]. *All About Technical Analysis.* New York: McGraw-Hill.

Brown, Constance [1999]. *Technical Analysis for the Trading Professional.* New York: McGraw-Hill.

Bulkowski, Thomas N. [2002]. *Trading Classic Chart Patterns.* New York: John Wiley & Sons. pp. 69-70. Protect a profit, minimize a loss, time loss, and maximize your use of capital.

Bulkowski, Thomas N. [2000]. *Encyclopedia of Chart Patterns.* New York: John Wiley & Sons.

Chande, Tushar S. [2001]. *Beyond Technical Analysis 3rd Edition.* New York: John Wiley & Sons.

Colby, Robert and Thomas Meyers [2002]. *Encyclopedia of Market Indicators.* New York: McGraw-Hill.

Dobson, Edward D. [1985] *Understanding Fibonacci Numbers.* Greenville, SC: Traders Press, Inc.

Dorsey, Thomas, J. *Point and Figure Charting 2nd Edition.* New York: John Wiley & Sons. Excellent book on point and figure charting.

Edwards, Robert D. and John Magee [2001]. *Technical Analysis of Stock Trends 8th Edition.* New York: AMACOM.

Eng, William F. [1988]. *Technical Analysis of Stocks, Options and Futures*. New York: McGraw-Hill.

Fischer Robert [2001]. *The New Fibonacci Trader Workbook.* New York: John Wiley & Sons.

Fischer, Robert [1993]. *Fibonacci Applications and Strategies for Traders.* New York: John Wiley & Sons.

Frost, Alfred J. and Robert Prechter, Jr. [1999]. *Elliott Wave Principle.* New York: John Wiley & Sons.

Graham, Benjamin and David L. Dodd [1996]. *Security Analysis: The Classic 1934 Edition.* New York: McGraw-Hill.

Harris, L [1986]. *A Transaction Data Study of Weekly and Intraday Patterns in Stock Returns.* Journal of Financial Economics, 16, 99-117.

Hobbs, Derrik S. [2003]. *Fibonacci for the Active Trader.* Los Angeles, CA: TradingMarkets. Excellent clearly written, easy to understand.

Hoggart, V.E., Jr. and Majorie Bicknell-Johnson [1979]. *Reflections Across Two and Three Glass Panes.* The Fibonacci Quarterly, 17, (April), 118-142

Jenkins, Michael S. [1992]. *The Geometry of Stock Market Profits.* Greenville, SC: Traders Press, Inc. Excellent book on the geometry of trading including proportion and harmony, and impulse waves.

Luca, Cornelius [1997]. *Technical Analysis Applications in the Global Currency Markets.* New York: New York Institute of Finance. Overview of technical analysis for every market.

Merrill, Arthur [1983]. *Filtered Waves.* Chappaqua NY: Analysis Press.

Morris, Gregory L. [1992]. *Candlestick Charting Explained.* Chicago: Irwin Professional Publishing.

Murphy, John [2002]. *Technical Analysis of the Financial Markets 2nd Edition.* New York: Putnam Press.

Nison, Steve [2001]. *Japanese Candlestick Charting Techniques 2nd Edition.* New York: New York Institute of Finance

Nison, Steve [1994]. *Beyond Candlesticks.* New York: John Wiley & Sons.

Prechter, Jr. Robert R. and Alfred J. Frost [2000]. *Elliott Wave Principle.* Gainesville, GA: New Classics Library.

Prechter, Jr., Robert T. *Fibonacci-Based Fractal Form and Elliott Waves.* Technical Analysis of Stocks and Commodities. 21, 9 (September), 74-77.

Pring, Martin J. [2002]. *Technical Analysis Explained 4th Edition.* New York: McGraw-Hill.

Pring, Martin J. [2002]. *How to Select Stocks Using Technical Analysis.* New York: McGraw-Hill.

Pring Martin J. [2002]. *Candlesticks Explained.* New York: McGraw-Hill.

Wheelan, Alexander H. [2004]. *Study Helps in Point and Figure Technique.* Greenville, SC: Traders Press, Inc. Reprint of original 1947 book.

FIBONACCI WEBSITES ON REFLECTIONS ACROSS GLASS PANES

Easier Fibonacci Puzzles (p.11).   http://www.mcs.surrey.ac.uk/Personal/R.Knott/Fibonacci/
fibpuzzles.html.

Information on Fibonacci Sequences (p.3). http://www.schoolnet.ca/vp-pv/amof/e_fibol.htm

Eric Weisstein's Mathematics (p.2). http://mathworld.wolfram.com/FibonacciNumber.html.

CHARTING SERVICES

"Traders' Resource: Data Services" [2004]. *Technical Analysis of Stocks & Commodities.* <u>22</u>, 11,
(November).
Extensive list of data services.

JOURNALS LISTED ALPHABETICALLY

<u>Active Trader</u>

Active Trader Magazine
P.O. Box 567
Mt. Morris, IL 61054-0567
(800)341-9384
www.activetradermag.com

Available in most major bookstores and newsstands and by subscription.

<u>Futures</u>

P.O. Box 2122
Skokie, IL 60076-7822
(888)-804-6612
www.futures.com

Available in most bookstores and newsstands and by subscription.

<u>SFO: Stocks Futures Options</u>

Wassendorf & Associates
P.O. Box 849
Cedar Falls, IA 50613
www.sfomag.com

Available in bookstores and newsstands in financial areas and by subscription.

<u>Technical Analysis of Stocks & Commodities</u>

(800)832-4642

E-mail: circ@traders.com

www.traders.com

Available in most bookstores and newsstands and by subscription.

<u>Tradersworld</u>

Halliker's, Inc.
2508 Grayrock St.
Springfield, MO 65810
www.tradersworld.com

Available in most bookstores and newsstands and by subscription.

CHAPTER FIVE

POSITION AND RISK MANAGEMENT

POSITION MANAGEMENT BASICS

A switch trade involves three instruments; options, a single stock future, and the underlying stock. This makes the switch trade one of the most complex trades to execute properly. Therefore, a brief discussion of position and risk management seems in order. Simply put, the basic goals of position management are:

- minimize losses,
- protect profits and
- maximize your use of capital.

Another reason for a consideration of position management is the most important price on any chart. What is the most important price on any chart? It is not the open. It is not the close. It is not the high. It is not the low. The most important price on any chart is the price that you paid for your stock or option. It goes like this. You purchase a stock or option. Then, you watch the market challenge your position with every tick. Furthermore, the more people who buy a stock at a given price, or within a given price range, the more investors there are who are emotionally committed to that level.

Conventional wisdom holds that four pieces of information are needed before initiating a trade:

1. How much am I willing to lose on the trade? (How much can I afford to lose?)
2. What is the target price(s)? (How much can I afford to win?)
3. What price am I willing to pay?
4. How long do I expect to hold the position?

The first two questions are used to calculate a reward/risk ratio. How much you are willing to lose provides an initial exit point in case you are wrong. The basic idea is: If you buy a stock and it goes down, you were wrong. If you were wrong the first time, what makes you think you will be correct the second time? Get out and re-evaluate. A target price answers the question: "Where do I expect the stock to go in terms of price?" There is also an implied second question which is often overlooked: "How much can I afford to win?" Any investor who has divided a portfolio into bonds, cash equivalents, large cap stocks and growth stocks has implicitly answered the question: "How much can I afford to win?" You can afford to win the amount you have in growth stocks. This question also helps answer how long a winner is permitted to run. Answers to the first two questions determine the reward/risk ratio. It can prove fatal to enter a trade without knowing this ratio. This is true whether you are making a day trade or investing in a 401K.

This chapter provides an approach to answer these four questions. The approach combines thirty years of experience, day trading experience since January, 2000 and ideas from sources and people too numerous to mention. Some of the more helpful resources are provided as references at the end of this chapter.

The components of position management are:
1. The Setup.
2. Trigger Event (usually more than one).
3. Entry Strategy
    o   Initial Protective Stop.
    o   Target Price and Time (usually more than one).
    o   Opening the Trade (Timing, Price and Order Type).
    o   Time Cancel. The length of time to leave an unexecuted entry order as a working order before canceling it.
    o   Initial Time Stop. The length of time before closing a position due to failure of the position to move in the expected direction.
4. Risk Management
    o   Potential Problem Areas in Terms of Price and Time.
    o   Trailing Protective Stops.
5. Exit Strategy.
6. Follow-up Action after Exiting Position.

SETUP

The setup places current events in perspective. As such, the setup provides the basis for identifying a trigger event and subsequent position management activities. It is always completed before a trading session begins. Beginning a trading session without first setting up the trading charts is like playing a tennis match without first drawing the boundary lines and then asking your opponent to be the judge, keep score and tell you who is winning. There is no one, best group of setups. The point is to develop a setup that meets your trading time frame, personality and risk-aversion style. Then use it before making any trade.

TRIGGER EVENT

A trigger event is some predetermined action or trading situation that will make you "pull the trigger" and open a trading position. The key is the word "predetermined." The type of trigger used depends on the trading style of the trader. Long-term trigger events differ from swing trading trigger events and swing trading trigger events differ from day trading trigger events. In addition, fundamental analysis trigger events differ from technical analysis trigger events.

Technical analysis trigger events include:
- The attainment of a specific price such as a 52-week high.
- A specific candlestick pattern such as a bullish engulfing pattern.
- A specific trading pattern such as a pennant or consolidation rectangle.
- A Fibonacci signal such as a 61.8 percent retracement.
- Technical signals such as crossing a moving average or a resistance level break-through.

The nature of specific trigger events is not important. The important point is to establish clearly-defined, predetermined, potential trading situations ahead of time. Trigger events serve two functions: (1) they tell you when to enter a trade and (2) they tell you when not to enter a trade. When not to enter a trade is as important as when to initiate a trade. Trigger events can be used to keep a trader out of a bad trade. For example:
- when the trigger event does not occur, don't even think about placing an order to open a position, or
- when surprised by an event that everyone says is a definite buy or sell signal, avoid the impulse to get on the bandwagon.

The rationale goes like this:
- When a trigger event does not occur, you know you have already made one mistake, *i.e.*, the trigger event has not happened. Therefore, don't compound your mistake by putting investment capital at risk when you don't know what you are doing.
- When surprised by an event, you are too late. The smart money has already gone long (or short). In this case, you are running the risk of finding yourself on the wrong side of the market.

Trigger events tell you when to place an order to open a position. They do not provide information about the entry strategy.

ENTRY STRATEGY

Initial Protective Stop (IPS)

An initial protective stop represents the maximum amount you are willing to lose on a trade if you are incorrect and the trade goes against you immediately. Some people might think this is a strange place to start an entry strategy. However this is the point from which everything else follows. For example, a trader could lose three percent of a portfolio twenty-two times in a row and still have 51.2 percent of the original portfolio. Even a ten percent loss could be considered acceptable by some traders. For example, a trader could lose ten percent of a portfolio six times in a row and still have 53.1 percent of the portfolio remaining. However as the consecutive loss percentage approaches twenty percent, the results become catastrophic. A trader who loses twenty percent of a portfolio three times in a row has 51.2 percent of the portfolio remaining. These examples could be considered an extreme case used to make a point. So, let's take another scenario. This is a trick question so be careful.

On a $1,000 investment, which would you rather have:
1. A fifty percent loss followed by an eighty percent gain or
2. A ten percent loss followed by a seven percent gain?

The answer is: You would be sixty-three dollars ahead with a ten percent loss followed by a seven percent gain.

Skeptics may say: "So what! You've still lost money." Let's take an illustration from poker to answer this question. If you sit at a poker table long enough, by pure blind luck, sooner or later, you will be dealt a winning hand with a big pot. If you have already lost your bankroll, you are no longer sitting at the table. Some other lucky sap will be sitting in your chair collecting the winnings. This situation is expressed in a well known stock market rule. Cut your losses quickly and let the winners run. The initial protective stop speaks to the first part of this rule.

Target Price and Timing

The target price is more difficult to determine than the initial protective stop because people are more used to asking the question: "How much can I afford to lose?" Some common reactions to the necessity of a target price before opening a position are: "How can I know that ahead of time?" or "I will let the market tell me when to take a profit." or "When you have doubled your money, sell half of your position." Why this factor is ignored, or swept under the rug, so often is difficult for me to understand. A target return is part of every other business investment decision. For example, what company would introduce a new product, buy a piece of capital equipment or make an acquisition decision without first determining a target return as part of a return on investment calculation?

A good way to set a target price is to use commonly accepted trading patterns with clearly stated targets. Some of these include pennants, head and shoulders patterns and measurement gaps. Two encyclopedic references for such patterns are Bulkowski[2000] and Colby and Meyers[2002]. Another generally accepted method for determining a target price is Fibonacci analysis. Several good sources on Fibonacci analysis are listed in the references at the end of this chapter.

The important point is, no matter how a trader does it, a target price is necessary before opening a trade.

Opening the Trade (Entry Timing, Entry Price and Order Type)

A brief overview of the types of orders is needed before going further. This discussion is meant to be a summary or overview. There are many types of orders. For an excellent summary of order types see Appendix A in Williams and Hoffman [2001]. Orders have three components: the price at which the order is executed, when and how the order is to be executed, and how long the order remains valid before it is cancelled.

There are three types of price orders: a limit order, a stop limit order, and a market order. A limit order says I am willing to buy (sell) this stock if I can buy (sell) it for this price or less (more). A stop limit order says I am willing to begin buying (selling) this stock when it hits this price but I am not willing to pay (sell for) more than (less than) this amount. A market order says I want to buy (sell) this stock as soon as possible no matter what the price.

When and how an order is executed and how long it remains valid are interrelated and need to be discussed together. A market on open is placed in a queue and is executed on open as soon as it reaches the front of the queue. A Fill or Kill order is either executed as soon as it hits the floor or else it is canceled. A Day order that has not been filled prior to close is canceled at the end of the trading day. A Good-Til-Cancel (GTC) order is ether filled during the day it is placed or carried over from day-to-day until it is physically canceled by the trader who placed it. Some brokerage houses cancel GTC orders after a certain time period or at the end of the month. Check with your brokerage house to find out how it handles GTC orders. Another type of order is the one-cancels-other order. This order is placed when a breakout is expected with the direction uncertain. Simultaneous buy long and sell short orders are placed. The buy long order is placed above the current market price and the sell short order is placed below the current market price. If the stock goes up the buy long order is executed. This action automatically cancels the sell short order. The filling of one order automatically cancels the other order, hence the name one-cancels-other or OCO. Not all firms provide this type of order. Be sure to check with your broker before trying to place this order.

Some order types are specific to option trading. Some, but not all, brokerage houses offer these orders. A contingent option order is an order to buy or sell an option based on the price of the underlying security. For example, a contingent order for IBM with a current market price of 89.55 might be: buy 10 IBM March 95 calls at market when the price of IBM reaches 91.05. This order would not be filled unless the price of IBM reaches the contingent price of 91.05. Another option-specific order is the net spread order. A net spread order might be: buy 10 MSFT March 25 calls and sell 10 MSFT March 30 calls for a net debit of 2.35. This order would not be filled unless the combination sale and purchase would generate a net debit of 2.35 or less.

With this background on order types, entry price can now be considered. For a long stock position, the entry price translates to the question: "How much am I willing to pay for this stock at this time?" This is an important consideration for most important purchases ranging from automobiles to houses. Why this is ignored so often with stocks is difficult to understand. An entry price must take into consideration the market conditions at the time the order is placed. An entry price is determined by the type of order placed, the reward/risk profile of the order and the reasons for using a particular type of order. For example, a market order means a trader goes long or short as quickly as possible without regard to the amount paid or received for the stock or option. This can sometimes prove disastrous when shorting a stock in a falling market because a stock can only be shorted on an up-tick. The result is, sometimes, shorting a stock into a falling market means your short order cannot be filled until the stock has stopped falling in price. In other words, you were correct but you lost money.

The main determinants of entry price are the planned initial protective stop and the target price. When the entry price is too high, the potential profit is definitely decreased because the entry price is closer than planned to the target price. Additionally, when the entry price is too high, the potential loss if you are wrong is greater than desired because the difference between the entry price and the initial protective stop is greater than desired.

TIME CANCEL

The logic behind deciding upon the length of time to leave an unexecuted entry order as a working order before canceling it goes like this. An order is placed because something is expected to begin happening in the near future. The definition of what constitutes "the near future" depends upon the time frame being traded. A trader using 3-minute charts obviously has a different definition of "the near future" than a long-term trader using daily and weekly charts.

The main point is, if something doesn't happen in the near future, the trader's timing expectations are incorrect. If timing expectations are incorrect, are price expectations also incorrect? Exit stage left and reanalyze the trade.

INITIAL TIME STOP

An initial time stop is the length of time that will be permitted to pass before closing a position due to failure to move in the expected direction. When a position does not move in the expected direction **and** when the initial protective stop is not hit, the stock has to be moving sideways. There are three reasons why a stock moves sideways: (1) it is consolidating its gains before continuing an up trend (or downtrend), (2) it is at a top (or bottom) and is preparing to reverse direction, or (3) it is entering a long-term, sideways trading zone. Carefully revaluate the rationale for opening the trade in light of the failure of the position to move in the expected direction. If the rationale is still valid set a new time stop. Otherwise exit the trade. Leaving investment funds tied up in a trade that is not performing according to expectations is poor money management.

RISK MANAGEMENT

Potential Problem Areas in Terms of Price and Time

Potential problem areas are time or price intervals placed between the initial protective stop and the target price. One of the most commonly asked questions about a stock is: "I bought XYZ for 32.50 three months ago. It is now at 41.75. Do you think I should sell now (time), or do you think it will go higher (price)?" This question is almost impossible to answer unless potential problem areas in terms of price and time are identified before a position is opened.

When a stock slows down at a potential problem area, instead of creating anxiety, it gives a trader confirmation that the original analysis was correct. Potential problem areas are critical to the second part of calmly cutting your losses quickly and letting the winners run. When a potential problem area is hit a trader has two alternatives: exit the position or set a trailing protective stop.

Trailing Protective Stops

A trailing protective stop is either a mental or actual stop order that is made with the intent of protecting some of the profit already generated. It is called a trailing stop because it trails the price of the stock as it moves in your direction. The purpose of trailing protective stops is to prevent a winning trade from becoming a losing trade. Trailing protective stops are placed at potential problem areas. Trailing protective stops are the trickiest and most difficult part of position management to execute properly.

The basic rationale for trailing protective stops is:

- Protect profits.
- Catch a free ride at the end of an uptrend or downtrend.
- Peace of mind and calm detachment. The decisions were made before the position was opened.
- When the position is going your way, a gain is guaranteed at little or no cost.
- The worst-case scenario is that you have made a profit.
- The downside is a trade is stopped out before it has a chance to meet the target. When there is a follow up plan, this is minimized because you can always get back in.

There is always the danger of a rapid decline past your protective stop. This could create losses that are larger than planned. Proper execution involves a balancing act between three stock market rules:

- Let your winners run.
- Never permit a profit to turn into a loss.
- No one ever went broke taking a profit.

Because a trader must be willing to exit at a trailing protective stop, it is often linked to the exit strategy.

EXIT STRATEGY

Exit orders are placed:

- when the target price is hit,
- when the market has moved too quickly in your favor and
- at the end of a predetermined holding period.

The purpose of an exit strategy is to collect gains when a trader makes a profitable trade. An exit order can be either mental or actual. The actual exit order is either a stop/limit order or a stop at market order that is placed below (for long positions) or above (for short positions) the current market price of a stock. Such an order is usually placed slightly below (above) a potential problem area. A mental exit order is not placed ahead of time. Instead, the trader carefully watches a stock and than places the closing exit order when the stock hits a certain level. The main advantage of a mental exit order for highly volatile stocks is a mental stop prevents being whipsawed out of a stock too soon. The main disadvantage of a mental stop is the human tendency to hold and hope too long. An actual stop exit order is already in the queue when the stock hits the trigger price and the personal emotional element is removed from the process. The trader does not have to think about the order. When the stop price is hit, the order is executed. The main disadvantage of the actual stop exit order is that it may be prematurely triggered by a fleeting, temporary down (up) tick. As a result the trader can be taken out of a long (or short) position in the middle of the up trend (downtrend) and thereby leave additional profits on the table. A good follow up strategy can minimize this loss by getting the trader back into the uptrend (downtrend).

FOLLOW-UP ACTION AFTER EXITING A POSITION

It is human nature to wonder what might have been. Developing a follow-up strategy for an exit point helps deal with this question in a constructive manner. A predetermined follow-up action at each potential problem area provides a re-entry point in case the stock keeps moving in the same direction or in case the stock reverses direction.

The logic goes like this:
- I have successfully determined the movement of the stock in the immediate past.
- I probably have a good chance of being correct again.
- Why not continue to trade this stock until I make a mistake?

Potential problem areas and targets provide intermediate points where, depending upon the circumstances, a position should be closed. An exit point determines when the trade should be closed without exception. The obvious question is: What happens when the stock keeps moving up (or down for a short position) after I have exited a position? This is the reason every position needs a clear exit point and a follow up strategy. The follow up actions also provide a starting point for a trade post mortem.

FIGURE **5.1** provides a form that has proven useful for position management. This form is filled out for every trade that is being considered. It is often instructive to compare both the trades that are not placed or executed with the trades that are placed.

The abbreviations on this form are explained below:
- XNF: Cancel if not filled time.
- Time Fill/XL: Time the opening order is filled or cancelled.
- L/S: L=Long: Open a position by purchasing the stock, option or single stock future.
    S= Short: Open a position by selling the stock, option or single stock future.
- IPS: Initial Protective Stop.
- TGT: Target.
- PA: Potential Problem Area.
- TPS: Trailing Protective Stop.
- Columns in the Comments Section.
    - Codes
        - TR: Trigger.
        - ST: Stop.
        - L: Limit.
        - TX: Time to cancel if position does not move in the expected direction.
        - IPS: Initial Protective Stop.
        - T1: Target 1.
        - Exit: Predetermined exit point.
        - TPS 2, TPS 3, TPS 4, *etc.*: Trailing Protective Stop 2, Trailing Protective Stop 3, Trailing Protective Stop 4, *etc.*
        - T2, T3, T4, *etc.*: Target 2, Target 3, Target 4, *etc.*
        - FWP. Follow up plan.
    - Second Column provides a place to tick off executed orders or when a price is hit for a chart pattern.
    - Time: The time an event occurred.
    - Chart/ Order#: Either type of chart used to identify a technical pattern (1-min, 5-min, daily, *etc.*) or the order number for a placed or executed transaction.
    - Comments: Rationale supporting the entry.

FIGURE 4.5: DIFFERENT LIGHT RAY PATHS THROUGH TWO PANES OF GLASS

	time identified	time placed	XNF time	time Fill/XL	price identifie	price placed	fill/XL price	potential gain	actual result

symbol	L/S		amount	stop	limit	time		amount	stop	limit	type	time
		u o ssf					IPS					
symbol	L/S		amount	stop	limit	time		amount	stop	limit	type	time
		u o ssf					IPS					
symbol	L/S		amount	stop	limit	time		amount	stop	limit	type	time
		u o ssf					IPS					

Target

price	time		price	time		price	time		price	time	
		u o ssf			u o ssf			u o ssf			u o ssf
price	time		price	time		price	time		price	time	
		u o ssf			u o ssf			u o ssf			u o ssf

PA		TPS		PA		TPS	

price	time	amount	stop	limit	type	price	time	amount	stop	limit	type
price	time	amount	stop	limit	type	price	time	amount	stop	limit	type
price	time	amount	stop	limit	type	price	time	amount	stop	limit	type
price	time	amount	stop	limit	type	price	time	amount	stop	limit	type

	amount	stop	limit	time	price placed	fill/XL price	time placed	XNF time	time Fill/XL
Exit Position 1 Follow Up									
Exit Position 2 Follow Up									
Exit Position 3 Follow Up									

code	time	price	chart/ order #	comments
TR				
ST				
L				
TX				
IPS				
T1				
Exit				
TPS 1				
TPS 2				
TPS 3				
TPS 4				
TPS 5				
TPS 6				
TPS 7				
TPS 8				
T2				
T3				
T4				
T5				
T6				
T7				
T8				
FWP				

Entering the time a potential trade was identified is good for two types of post mortems. The first use is to review chart patterns that resulted in profitable and unprofitable trades. The second use is to review those trades that you thought about but did not make because you either failed to pull the trigger or canceled the trade before it was executed. This can sometimes prove more valuable than information on trades that were actually executed.

The price when identified coupled with the time between identification and the time when the trade was placed helps make you a more decisive and accurate trader. The difference between the time and price at which the trade was placed and executed helps evaluate your broker. On an actively traded stock, I consider an average time difference greater than ten seconds as unacceptable. On most actively traded stocks, I find an average slippage greater than two cents unacceptable. Slippage is the difference between the price of the stock at which the order was entered and the price paid for the stock. You will usually find the time of execution directly related to slippage. These two factors are of primary importance to successful traders. Commissions and management fees are important. However, they are not as important as execution time and slippage. For example, an average slippage of twenty cents represents two hundred dollars on 1,000 shares. A brokerage house that charges nine dollars per trade and has an average slippage of twenty cents per trade is, in fact, costing you two hundred and nine dollars a trade. I have, personally, experienced slippage fees as high as sixty cents or six hundred dollars on one trade on a highly volatile stock. Important items to consider when placing a trade are the open interest on the options and single stock future and the volume of the options and the underlying. Generally, the higher the open interest and volume the better the execution in terms of time and price.

In Figure 5.1, there are three entry lines for opening positions. The first entry is the symbol for the underlying, the option, or the single stock future. Room to enter three opening positions permits the use of butterfly spreads. The second entry is a place to write "l" for a long position or "s" for a short position. The third entry area has the codes "u" for underlying which means a stock, index, etc., "o" for option, and "ssf" for single stock future. The trigger event could be a price level or a technical event such as breaking a resistance level or reaching a Fibonacci trading zone. Next to the open data is the IPS or initial protective stop data. This includes the "type" of IPS meaning a mental or an actual stop.

The target section has room for eight different target prices and times. This is usually overkill but sometimes comes in handy when using Fibonacci or Elliott Wave analysis.

Problem Areas (PA) and Trailing Protective Stops (TPS) are included together. In practice, I have found it useful to use trailing protective stops as potential problems areas are approached. An actual protective stop is placed before the stop price is reached. A mental protective stop is not placed until a predetermined price is reached. Deciding before hand, where and when and how to place protective stops, reduces anxiety. Post mortem analysis of these decisions helps decide when and how far to let a winner run.

CONCLUSION

The four questions to be answered before initiating a trade are:
1. How much am I willing to lose on the trade? (How much can I afford to lose?)
2. What is the target price or prices? (How much can I afford to win?)
3. What price am I willing to pay?
4. How long do I expect to hold the position?

A six step process for answering these four questions was provided and discussed. The six step position management process is:
1. The Setup.
2. Trigger Event. (Usually more than one.)
3. Entry Strategy.
4. Position and Risk Management.
5. Exit Strategy.
6. Follow-up Action after Exiting a Position.

The calendar spread in Chapter Six is used to illustrate position management.

REFERENCES

Chart Patterns as Price Targets

Bigalow, Steven W. [2002]. *Profitable Candlestick Trading.* New York: John Wiley & Sons.

Bollinger, John [2002]. *Bollinger on Bollinger Bands.* New York: McGraw-Hill.

Bulkowski, Thomas N. [2002]. *Trading Classic Chart Patterns.* New York: John Wiley & Sons. pp. 69-70 Protect a profit, minimize a loss, time loss, maximize your use of capital.

Bulkowski, Thomas N. [2000]. *Encyclopedia of Chart Patterns.* New York: John Wiley & Sons.

Colby, Robert and Thomas Meyers [2002]. *Encyclopedia of Market Indicators.* New York: McGraw-Hill.

Dorsey, Thomas, J. *Point and Figure Charting 2nd Edition.* New York: John Wiley & Sons.

Fischer, Robert [2001]. *The New Fibonacci Trader Workbook.* New York: John Wiley & Sons.

Jenkins, Michael S. [1992]. *The Geometry of Stock Market Profits.* Greenville, SC: Traders Press, Inc.

Nison, Steve [2001]. *Japanese Candlestick Charting Techniques 2nd Edition.* New York: New York Institute of Finance

Nison, Steve [1994]. *Beyond Candlesticks.* New York: John Wiley & Sons.

Fibonacci Analysis

Fischer, Robert [2001]. *The New Fibonacci Trader Workbook.* New York: John Wiley & Sons.

Fischer, Robert [1993]. *Fibonacci Applications and Strategies for Traders.* New York: John Wiley & Sons.

Frost, Alfred J. and Robert Prechter, Jr. [2000]. *Elliott Wave Principle.* Gainesville, GA: New Classics Library.

Hobbs, Derrik S. [2003]. *Fibonacci for the Active Trader.* Los Angeles, CA: TradingMarkets.

Prechter, Jr., Robert T. "Fibonacci-Based Fractal Form and Elliott Waves." *Technical Analysis of Stocks and Commodities.* 21, 9 (September), 74-77.

Stevens, Leigh [2002]. *Essential Technical Analysis.* New York: John Wiley & Sons.
Fibonacci pp. 129-131, Gann pp. 309-319, Elliott Wave pp. 319-329.

Position Management, Types of Orders, Risk Management
Bernstein, Jake [1998]. *The Compleat Day Trader II.* New York: McGraw-Hill.
Bernstein, Jake and Elliot Bernstein [2002]. *Stock Market Strategies That Work.* New York: McGraw-Hill. Five Reasons to Keep Things Simple. Position Management.
Brown, Constance [2002]. *All About Technical Analysis.* New York: McGraw-Hill.
Cassidy, Donald L. *It's When you Sell that Counts.* New York: McGraw-Hill.
Dalton, John M. [2001]. *How The Stock Market Works 3rd Edition.* New York: New York Institute of Finance. Market and transaction mechanics.
Eng, William F. [1993]. *The Day Trader's Manual.* New York: John Wiley & Sons.
Eng, William F. [1988]. *Technical Analysis of Stocks, Options and Futures.* New York: McGraw-Hill.
Farrell, C.A. [1999]. *Day Trader Online.* New York: John Wiley & Sons.
Bid/Ask specialist.
Fosback, Norman G. [1994]. *Stock Market Logic.* Chicago: Dearborn Press.
Gallea, Anthony M. [2002]. *Bulls Make Money – Bears Make Money – Pigs Get Slaughtered.* New York: New York Institute of Finance.
Gonzalez, F. and W. Rhee [1999]. *Strategies for the Online Day Trader.* New York: McGraw-Hill.
Harris, L [1986]. *A Transaction Data Study of Weekly and Intraday Patterns in Stock Returns.* Journal of Financial Economics, 16, 99-117.
Kaufman, Perry J. [1998]. *Trading Systems and Methods 3rd Edition.* New York: John Wiley & Sons.
Jenkins, Michael S. [1992]. *The Geometry of Stock Market Profits.* Greenville, SC: Traders Press, Inc.
Excellent for position and risk management.
Leizman, Jon [2002]. *Short-Term Trading, Long-Term Profits.* New York: McGraw-Hill.
Overnight trades, trading strategies, trade mechanics, daily routine, bibliography.
Lukeman, Josh [2000]. *The Market Maker's Edge.* New York: McGraw-Hill.
Schlossberg, Boris [2004]. *What Happened to My Stop Loss?* Stocks Futures & Options. 3,1 (January), pp. 121 –122.
Paulos, John A. [2003]. *A Mathematician Plays the Stock Market.* New York: Basic Books.
Pring, Martin J. [2003]. *Technician's Guide to Day and Swing Trading.* New York: McGraw-Hill.
Sheimo, Michael D. [1999]. *Stock Market Rules.* New York: McGraw-Hill.
Taylor, France [2000]. *Mastering Derivative Markets 2nd Edition.* New York: Prentice-Hall. Accounting for derivatives.
Trester, Kenneth R. [2002]. *The Complete Options Player 4th Edition.* Lake Tahoe, NY: Institute for Options Research.
Velez, Oliver and Greg Capra [2000]. *Tools and Tactics for the Master Day Trader.* New York: McGraw-Hill.
Williams, Michael S., and Amy Hoffman [2001]. *Fundamentals of the Options Market.* New York: McGraw-Hill.
See Appendix A for a summary of order types.
Zelkin, Marvin H. [2002]. *It's Your Option: A Trader's Primer.* Greenville, SC: Traders Press, Inc.

CHAPTER SIX

CALENDAR SPREADS

OVERVIEW OF CALENDAR SPREADS

A calendar or time spread is so named because two options with different expiration, or "calendar," dates are used to construct the spread. A debit call calendar spread uses a long-term call option, usually six months or more, to cover the short sale of a shorter-term call option that has a strike equal to or greater than the longer-term option. There are two approaches for generating profits from a calendar spread.

- The most common use of the calendar spread is to take advantage of the different rate of time decay between the longer-term option and the shorter-term option. The more rapid time decay of the shorter-term option widens the spread so the spread can be closed at a profit.
- In the second approach, the debit incurred from the purchase of the longer-term option is offset by selling two or more shorter-term options, thereby, locking-in a guaranteed profit and generating writing income similar to a covered call.

The first approach to calendar spreads is the one most widely used. The basic expectation is that time decay will erode the value of the shorter-term option faster than the longer-term option. When this happens, the spread will become greater and a profit will occur. The goal of the first approach is to take advantage of the difference in the time decay between the two options. The second approach has the added goal of generating writing income by creating a situation similar to a covered call without having to assume the downside risk of the long stock position. The long option serves as protection for the shorter-term option. The expectation is that the shorter-term option will expire worthless and the same longer-term option will serve as protection for another short position. When properly executed, the long-term option can be used to cover several short positions thus generating profitable writing income over the life of the longer-term option. Because the longer-term option always costs more than the shorter-term option, the position always results in a net debit when it is first opened. However, subsequent short positions written against the original longer-term option always result in a net credit equal to the amount received for the short call. This is because the longer-term call was debited when the original position was opened.

55

There are two variations of calendar debit call spreads, *i.e.*, diagonal and horizontal calendar spreads. A diagonal calendar debit call spread involves buying a longer-term call and selling a shorter-term call with a strike price that is greater than the strike of the long-term option. A horizontal calendar debit call spread involves buying a longer-term call and selling a shorter-term call with both options having the same strike price. There are two types of horizontal spreads. (1) At-the-money strikes are used when the underlying is expected to move sideways during the life of the shorter-term option. (2) The next available out-of-the-money strike is used when the underlying is expected to drift higher during the life of the shorter-term option.

> Diagonal Spread Variations
> - Diagonal Calendar Spread.
>   Purchase long-term call.
>   Sell short-term call with a strike greater than the long-term call.
> - Horizontal Calendar Spread.
>   — Neutral Outlook.
>   Purchase long-term, at-the-money call.
>   Sell short-term at-the-money call.
>   — Slightly Bullish Outlook.
>   Purchase long-term slightly out-of-the-money call.
>   Sell short-tem call with same strike as the purchased call.

The horizontal calendar spread is used when the stock is expected to move sideways for the life of the shorter-term option. The diagonal spread is used when the underlying is expected to increase slightly in value over the life of the short-term option. This is not a strategy of choice when the stock is expected to decline in value.

A calendar spread is used to take advantage of the different rates of time decay between the longer-term option and the shorter-term option. However, the fact that the fair value of a single stock future does not experience time decay and does not depend upon volatility opens up interesting possibilities beyond time decay considerations. For example, a switch spread can take advantage of both time decay and an anticipated change in volatility. This can substantially increase potential profit.

Although the debit calendar spread has a risk limited to the initial debit, the equivalent switch calendar spread has an unlimited loss down to zero of the underlying. Therefore, although this is not a book on position management, the calendar spread is discussed within the framework of position management that was discussed in Chapter Five. The purpose is to provide one detailed example as an illustration of the importance of position management when a switch spread is used. This is the only spread discussed in such detail.

The components of position management discussed in Chapter Five are:

1. The Setup.
2. Trigger Event. (Usually more than one.)
3. Entry Strategy.
   - Initial Protective Stop.
   - Target Price and Time. (Usually more than one.)
   - Opening the Trade (Entry Timing, Price and Order Type.)
   - Time Cancel - The length of time to leave an unexecuted entry order as a working order before canceling it.
   - Initial Time Stop - The length of time before closing a position due to failure to move in the expected direction.
4. Risk Management.
   - Potential Problem Areas in terms of price and time.
   - Trailing Protective Stops.
5. Exit Strategy.
6. Follow-up Action after Exiting Position.

HORIZONTAL CALENDAR SPREAD

SETUP

Figure 6.1 provides a weekly chart for Hewlett Packard, Co. (HPQ) containing some of the technical analysis and setup lines used for the HPQ calendar spread. Figure 6.1 gives a long-term look at HPQ using a weekly chart. It provides an excellent example of a downtrend with the three major trading gaps: a breakaway gap (top arrow), a measurement gap (middle arrow) and an exhaustion gap (bottom arrow). A breakaway down gap occurs at the top of an up trend and signals the beginning of a major reversal. A measurement gap occurs at the midpoint of a trend and signals the continuation of the trend with a target end point equal to the distance from the top of the trend to the measurement gap. In this case the target end point is near 15.00. An exhaustion gap is the last gap, or gasp, of a trend. It signals either a reversal or a consolidation period with the stock moving sideways for a period of time. When the exhaustion gap is quickly filled, but not exceeded, there is a high probability of a period of consolidation or sideways movement. Gap or window analysis is an important tool in the technical analysis toolbox. Most books on technical analysis contain a discussion of the use of gaps (see Chapter Four).

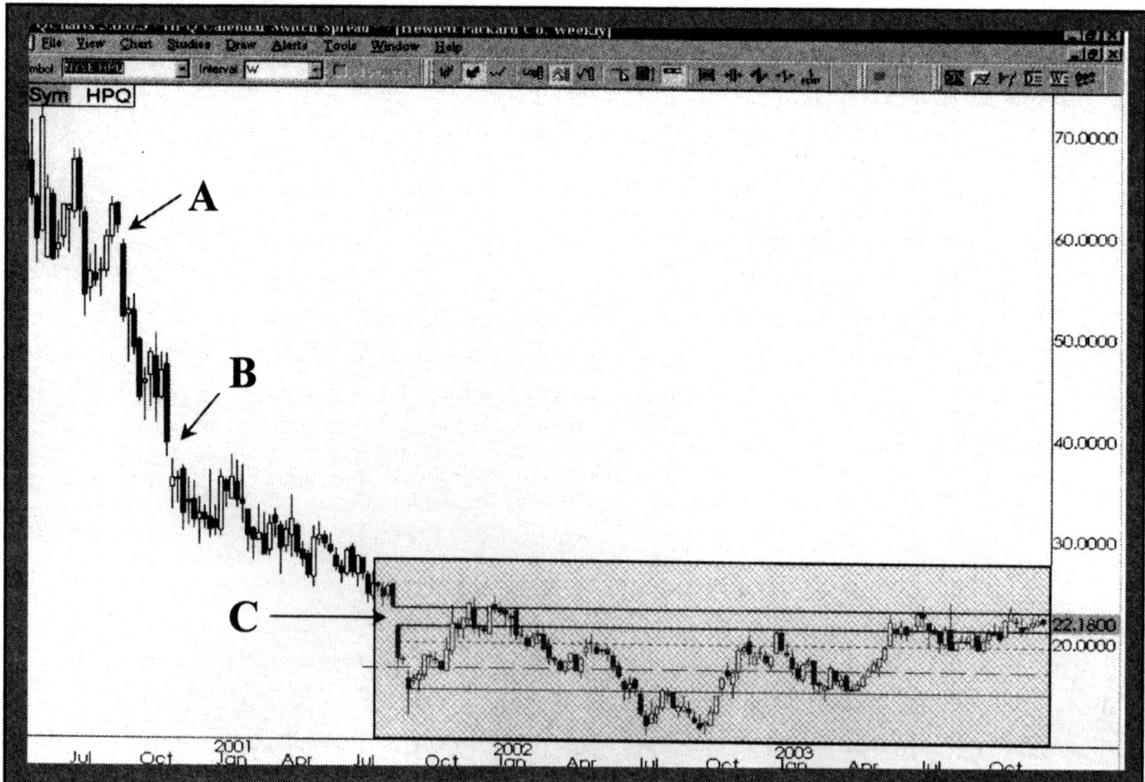

In **FIGURE 6.1**, the top arrow (A) points to the breakaway gap, the middle arrow (B) points to the measurement gap, and the bottom arrow (C) points to the exhaustion gap. The gray area is used for short-term analysis and detailed set up lines. This area is shown Figure 6.2.

FIGURE 6.2:

The arrow in **FIGURE 6.2** points out the exhaustion gap. The distance from top of the gap (the top solid line) to bottom of the gap (the second solid line) is an important price zone. Candlestick analysis refers to this as a trading window. As long as the price does not break the high of this zone, the stock will not experience a significant reversal. The fact that HPQ simply fills the gap and does not break the top of the trading window provides evidence of strong resistance at 23.01 which is the top solid line. The "W" bottom (the oval in Figure 6.2) indicates the probable end of the downtrend. If HPQ breaks a line drawn from the middle of the "W" bottom then it will probably go down to at least the bottom of the "W" at 11.96. The fact that the downtrend reverses at the middle of the "W" bottom plus the fact that support forms at this line after the formation of the "W" Bottom helps confirm support at 15.40 represented by the long solid line at the bottom of the chart. The next step is to determine interior crossover support to resistance lines. This is the price (or prices) between support and resistance at which cross over resistance to support and temporary reversal points should form. In this

59

case the dotted line at the midpoint of the long black bar following the exhaustion gap provides one logical candidate. For an explanation of the use of long black and long white bodies to identify potential support and resistance see Chapter Four and Nison [1994]. Examination of Figure 6.2 results in a second such line that is based on the weekly chart in Figure 6.1, the dashed line at 17.50.

The setup is now complete. A consolidation zone with a top of 23.01 and a bottom of 15.40 has been identified. Temporary stopping and reversal points within this zone have been identified at 17.50 (the dashed line) and 19.61 (the dotted line). The exact setup lines used will vary from trader to trader. The main point is the setup lines have been drawn before the trade is executed. We are now ready to move to the trigger event for both the option calendar spread and the equivalent switch calendar spread.

Trigger Event

A good time trigger for a calendar spread is between one and two weeks after the last expiration Friday. Another trigger is a spread that generates a net debit that is less than fifty percent of the difference between adjacent strikes. A 17.50 strike for both calls meets this criteria. A third trigger is a technical formation with a clearly defined sideways range. Finally, the spread is opened when the underlying is expected to trade sideways in the near term and then increase significantly in the intermediate or long-term — not to exceed six months. This permits time decay to affect the price of the shorter-term short call. This situation occurred with Hewlett Packard, Co. (HPQ) on Friday, March 28, 2003. The option calendar spread is opened for a debit of 1.20.

Option Calendar Debit Spread
Buy November 17.50 Call	(1.90)	
Sell May 17.50 Call	0.70	
Net Debit	(1.20)	

The implied volatility of the long option is greater than the historical volatility of the underlying stock and the implied volatility of the short option is twelve percent higher than the implied volatility of the long option. This situation provides a good horizontal calendar spread opportunity because both implied volatility and time decay could work in your favor.

Volatilities
- HPQ Stock 20-day Annualized Volatility   0.380
- November 17.50 Call Implied Volatility   0.449
- May 17.50 Call Implied Volatility   0.505

The equivalent switch calendar spread is opened for a net credit of 0.74.

Switch Calendar Spread
HPQ Close	16.25	
Buy December Single Stock Future	16.21	
Single Stock Future "Premium"		0.04
Sell May 17.50 Call		0.70
Net Credit		0.74

The fair value of the HPQ December 2003 single stock future is 0.04 less than the underlying price of 16.25. This is not a mistake. This does occur. When the single stock future sells at a discount to the underlying, the result is an unplanned bonus. The main advantage of the switch spread is the switch spread starts with a net credit of 0.74 while the option spread starts with a net debit of 1.20. This means the switch calendar spread starts at 0.74 in-the-money while the underlying must increase to 18.70 before the option calendar spread starts making money. The underlying can decrease to 15.51 before the switch spread starts to lose money.

Breakeven Points
- Option Spread
        Strike of November 17.50 Option   17.50
        plus Net Debit   1.20
                    Option Spread BEP   18.70
- Switch Spread
        Market Price of HPQ   16.25
        minus Net Credit   0.74
                    Switch Spread BEP   15.51

The disadvantage of the switch spread is the possibility of the unlimited loss of the single stock future compared to a maximum loss of 1.20 of the option spread. The potential unlimited loss can be managed with proper position management techniques.

Maximum Potential Loss
- Option Spread
        Net Debit   1.20
- Switch Spread
        December Single Stock Future   Unlimited to Zero for HPQ

The switch calendar spread starts 0.74 in-the-money while the option calendar spread starts 2.45 out-of-the-money. This provides the opportunity to exit the switch spread at a small gain if the position moves against you. The option debit spread does not offer this alternative.

Initial In-The-Money Status
- Option Spread In-The-Money Status
        Option Spread BEP   18.70
        minus HPQ Close   16.25
            Option Spread In-The-Money Status   (2.45)
- Switch Spread In-The-Money Status
        HPQ Close   16.25
        minus Switch Spread BEP   15.51
            Switch Spread In-The-Money Status   0.74

Another consideration is the point at which the switch spread loss equals the option spread maximum potential loss. This price is 14.31.

- Point at Which Switch Spread Loss Equals Option Spread Loss.

Switch Calendar Spread BEP	15.51	
minus Net Debit of Option Spread	<u>1.20</u>	
Switch Loss Equals Option Loss		14.31

The 14.31 price is below a major support line in Figure 6.2. Barring (i) a major downdraft or (ii) excessive slippage, an initial stop placed slightly above this point provides a downside risk equal to the option spread. This process is part of the entry strategy.

Entry Strategy

Initial Protective Stop or Close ~ Protective stops for spreads are really conditional orders to close an open position. They can be placed on either the price of the option or the option can be closed based on the price of the underlying. The discussion of the initial protective stop and trailing protective stops assumes the trader has a brokerage house that supports closing option positions based on the price of the underlying stock. If your broker does not provide this alternative, seriously consider finding one that does. In Figure 6.2, the top of the "W" reversal formation in the "W" bottom (15.40) represents an excellent initial protective stop for both parts of the spread (Figure 6.2). HPQ could decrease to retest support at 15.40 before expiration of the short May option on Friday May 16, 2003. If support holds an increase in price to test the one-year high and bottom of the down gap at 21.30 is probable. At the minimum, an increase to 19.61 or 21.25 is possible. The rationale is: if the analysis is correct, after a brief pause, HPQ is ready to increase in price. If HPQ does not increase in price, then the analysis is incorrect and the trade should be exited because a continuation of the downtrend could occur to at least the bottom of the "W" pattern at 11.96. At the initial protective stop of 15.40, the loss for the option calendar spread is 1.20 plus the cost of buying back the short May call and transaction costs. The loss for the switch spread is 0.11 plus the cost of buying back the short May call and transaction costs. Admittedly, both positions have lost money. However, there is a considerable difference in the dollar amount of the loss.

Target Price and Time ~ If support holds, a rise to 21.30 is probable. This represents a test of the one-year high and the bottom of the down gap. The test could easily occur before the long option expires on Friday, November 21, 2003.

Opening the Trade (Timing, Price and Order Type)
- Option Calendar Spread. It is important to open the long option spread for a net debit rather than purchasing each option separately or "legging" into the spread. The analysis of the switch spread is based on a specific net debit for the option calendar spread. Entering the spread by purchasing each option separately will most certainly result in a different net debit. If your broker does not support net debit and net credit option spreads then either avoid this spread or change brokers.
- Switch Calendar Spread. It is important to purchase the December single stock future first. If this is not done, then a naked call position is created with all the attendant unlimited risks and account balance and margin requirements. A limit order is used to open the single stock future because the analysis of the switch spread is based on a specific price for the single stock future.

Unless the May 17.50 option has decreased significantly, a market order can be used to open the short option. If the short May 17.50 option cannot be sold at an advantageous price, consider closing or offsetting the long single stock future.

Time Cancel ~ (The length of time to leave an unexecuted entry order as a working order before canceling it.)
- Option Calendar Spread. The time taken to fill the opening order is not a consideration, as long as, it is filled the day it is placed. This is not a problem for the option calendar spread because the option spread is opened for a fixed net debit. The price paid for each leg of the spread is not important, as long as, the spread is opened for the target net debit.
- Switch Calendar Spread. If the long single stock future order is not filled quickly (say between thirty and sixty seconds) cancel the order. The reason for the quick cancel is that every second that passes increases the possibility that the price of the short option will decrease in value. If your brokerage house does not execute orders this quickly, either avoid the switch calendar spread or change brokers.

Initial Time Stop ~ (The length of time before closing a position due to failure to move in the expected direction.)
- Option Calendar Spread. With the option calendar spread, time is your friend because time decay quickly erodes the value of the short May 17.50 call while time decay has almost no impact on the long November 17.50 call. If HPQ moves sideways until the May 17.50 expires, there are two alternatives: (i) close the long November 17.50 call or (ii) open a new short option to further reduce the cost of the long November call.
- Switch Calendar Spread. When HPQ moves sideways until the May 17.50 expires worthless, seriously consider closing the December single stock future.

The reason for the difference between the option calendar spread and the switch spread is the single stock future leg of the switch spread can experience a loss if the underlying declines while the option calendar spread has a loss that is fixed at the initial net debit. Therefore, for the option calendar spread, opening a new short option reduces risk while increasing potential gain. The same situation is not the case for the switch calendar spread.

Risk Management

Potential Problem Areas in Terms of Price and Time ~ There are five potential problem areas:
1. The solid line at 15.40 representing the end of the downtrend, the middle of the "W" bottom, and a support level formed between January and April of 2003.
2. The dashed line representing the 17.50 position strikes and a crossover area identified on the weekly chart in Figure 6.1.
3. The dotted line at 19.61 representing the midpoint of a long black bar.
4. The solid line at 21.23 representing the bottom of the exhaustion gap.
5. The solid line at 23.01 representing the top of the exhaustion gap and the anticipated top of the sideways trading range.

Potential Problem Area 1 (PA1) is dealt with by the Initial Protective Stop. Problem Area 2 at 17.50 is a problem area because exercise of the short call becomes a possibility when HPQ moves above the strike at 17.50. Problem Area 3 (19.61) is a problem area because it represents a possible resistance and reversal area. Also if Problem Area 3 is broken the next stopping point is probably 21.23 which means the short 17.50 call becomes 3.73 in the money. This is a problem because, once the short 17.50 call reaches parity, it will almost certainly be exercised. When the solid line at 21.23, Problem Area 4, is broken the short 17.50 call position is in serious danger of being exercised.

Trailing Protective Stops or Closes ~ The purpose of trailing protective stops is to prevent a winning trade from becoming a losing trade.
- Option Calendar Spread – Long November 17.50 Call - Short May 17.50 Call. The maximum loss is set at the original net debit. The exit strategy provides for exiting at a profit. Therefore, there are few opportunities for trailing protective stops with the option calendar spread. It is possible to micromanage a trade.
- Switch Calendar Spread – Long December Single Stock Future – Short May 17.50 Call. The fact that the price of a single stock future closely parallels the price of the underlying makes trailing protective stops a useful tool. As long as you do not have trouble pulling the trigger when a stop is hit, mental stops are preferable because they prevent being whipsawed out of a profitable position. In this case, trailing protective stops would be set at the potential problem areas of 17.50, 19.61, 21.25 and 23.01.

Exit Strategy
Exit strategies are provided for both the option spread and the switch spread.
- Option Calendar Spread
  1. Close the short call when its value reaches 0.10 and leave the long November 17.50 open, as long as, HPQ closes above 15.40. This situation occurred consistently between April 21, 2003 and April 28, 2003. The rationale is at least half of the analysis worked and a profit is made on the short leg of the spread. Leaving the long November 17.50 open provides the opportunity to make a profit on both legs of the spread. There is also the possibility of using the long call to cover another shorter-term call at an equal or higher strike.
  2. Close the long November 17.50 Call when it reaches parity. Parity is a situation in which the strike price plus the premium is equal to the price of the underlying. This situation occurred during the day on July 15, 2000. The rationale is that the profit potential of the long call has been maximized. If you are still bullish on the underlying, purchase a higher strike call with part of the proceeds from the sale of the November 17.50 call.

When the option calendar spread position is managed as described above, the result is a net gain of 4.60 before transaction costs.

HPQ Option Calendar Spread Total Gain
- Purchased November 17.50 call

Opening Price	(1.90)	
Closing Price	5.90	
Gain from Nov 17.50 call		4.00

- Sold May 17.50 call

Opening Price	0.70	
Closing Price	(0.10)	
Gain from May 17.50 call		0.60
TOTAL GAIN FROM OPTION SPREAD		4.60

- Switch Calendar Spread ~ To provide a benchmark the switch calendar spread is handled in a manner that is equivalent to the option calendar spread.
  1. Close the short call when its value reaches 0.10 and leave the long December single stock future open, as long as, HPQ closes above 15.40. This situation occurred consistently between April 21, 2003 and April 28, 2003. The rationale is that at least half of the analysis worked and a profit is made on the short leg of the spread. Leaving the long December single stock future open provides the opportunity to make a profit on both legs of the spread. There is also the possibility of using the long December single stock future to cover another short-term, at-the-money or out-of-the-money call. However, the switch calendar spread needs a trailing protective stop on the long single stock future that is left open because of the potential loss of the long single stock future.
  2. Close the long December single stock future on July 15, 2000. The rationale is that HPQ is testing the 23.01 high of the setup trading zone and will probably retreat back to at least 21.25 and maybe as low as 19.61. Sometimes the underlying does not reverse when expected. When this happens, the follow-up strategy provides a reentry point.

When the switch calendar spread position is managed as described above, the result is a net gain of 7.24 before transaction costs. The mechanics are provided below.

HPQ Switch Calendar Spread Total Gain
- Purchased December Single Stock Future

Opening Single Stock Future Price	(16.21)	
Closing Single Stock Future Price	22.85	
Gain from December Single Stock Future		6.64

- Sold May 17.70 call

Opening Price	0.70	
Closing Price	(0.10)	
Gain from May 17.50 call		0.60
TOTAL GAIN FROM SWITCH SPREAD		7.24

The switch calendar spread has a 57.4 percent greater gain than the option calendar spread.

Follow Up

(Writing Additional Calls against the Long, Long-Term Position)

The most common approach to a calendar spread is to take advantage of the more rapid time decay of the shorter-term option. I call this alternative the "time alternative." The shorter-term option is closed at a profit and the longer-term option is held with the expectation of an increase in the price of the underlying so the longer-term option can also be closed for a gain. Therefore, both legs of the spread can make money.

A second alternative is to offset the debit incurred from the purchase of the longer-term option by selling two or more shorter-term options, thereby, locking-in profit and generating writing income. I call this the "writing alternative" for calendar spreads because the long position is used as a surrogate for the long stock position of a covered write. This is a more aggressive approach. A major caveat is the trader must be careful the added gains adequately offset the additional transactions costs.

The switch spread is well adapted to the writing alternative because there is no initial debit. As a result, the additional short options decrease the basis of the long single stock future. In addition there is no strike price with which to be concerned. For example, in the HPQ example, if HPQ never reached 17.50 during the life of the November spread and closed at 17.50, the long November call would expire worthless. However, under the same set of circumstances, the single stock future would generate a gain of 1.29 (17.50 minus the original price of 16.21). The setup lines help provide guidance for management of the additional short calls. A summary of possible follow up actions using the writing alternative is provided below.

- Gains From Short Calls
    Original Short May 17.50 Call
        Opened 03/28/03   0.70
        Closed 04/21/03   (0.10)
                    Net Gain   0.60
    Second Short August 22.50 Call
        Opened 06/06/03   1.10
        Closed 04/21/03   (0.05)
                    Net Gain   1.05
    Third Short November 22.50 Call
        Opened 08/19/03   1.45
        Closed 08/25/03   (0.35)
                    Net Gain   1.10
        GAIN FROM ALL SHORT OPTIONS   2.75

- Gain From Long Option Part Of Option Calendar Spread
    Long November 17.50 call option.
        Opened 03/28/03   (1.90)
        Closed 11/07/03   5.50
    Gain from Long Nov 17.50 Call   3.60
    Writing Income from Short Options   2.75
    TOTAL GAIN FROM OPTION SPREAD   6.35

When the equivalent switch calendar spread is managed in this manner the gain from all of the short options remains the same at 2.75. When the gain from the single stock future that is switched for the long-term call option is added to the 2.75, the total for the switch spread is 9.39. The calculations are provided below.

Total Gain from Switch Spread
    Gain from Long December Single Stock Future (SSF) Part of Switch Calendar Spread
        Long December Single Stock Future
            Opened 03/28/03   (16.21)
            Closed 11/07/03   22.85
            Gain from Long December SSF   6.64
    Writing Income from Short Options   2.75
    TOTAL GAIN FROM SWITCH SPREAD   9.39

The time alternative for the option calendar spread generated a net gain of 4.60 while the writing alternative for the option calendar spread generated a trading gain of 6.35. The time alternative for the switch calendar spread generated 7.24 while the writing alternative for the switch calendar spread generated 9.39. The switch version of the calendar spread performed better for both the time and the writing alternatives. An additional consideration is that the single stock future would have provided an additional profit if HPQ had broken out to an uptrend.

CONCLUSION

A calendar or time spread uses two options with different expiration, or calendar, dates. The debit call calendar spread uses a longer-term call option, usually six months or more, to cover the short sale of a shorter-term call option that has a strike equal to or greater than the longer-term option. Two approaches for generating profits from calendar spreads are discussed. The first, most widely used, alternative is called the time alternative because it is based on the difference in time decay between the short, shorter-term call option and the long, longer-term option. The second alternative, called the writing alternative, takes advantage of the difference in time decay while adding the additional feature of using the long call to create additional covered write alternatives. With a switch calendar spread, my feeling is that as long as the underlying performs like a good child and follows the rules and lines drawn in the setup; continue to open new short positions. Some traders will decide the extra risks and transaction costs are not worth the extra potential gains.

This chapter begins a discussion of the spread strategies. Therefore, the differences between an option calendar spread and a switch calendar spread were drawn out in detail by using the framework for position management provided in Chapter Five. The remaining chapters do not contain as much detail about position management.

REFERENCES

Bigalow, Steve [2004]. "Market Timing with Candlesticks." *Technical Analysis of Stocks and Commodities,* 22, 5, pp. 88-90.

McClean, William [2003]. *Timing Events with the Calendar Spread.* Active Trader, 9, 10 (October), pp. 66-67.

McMillan, Lawrence G. [2002]. *Options as a Strategic Investment. 4th Edition.* New York: New York Institute of Finance.

Neal, Jeff [2003]. "Calendar Ratio Backspread." *Technical Analysis of Stocks and Commodities,* 21, 10 (October), pp. 58-61.

Nison, Steve [2001]. *Japanese Candlestick Charting Techniques 2nd Edition.* New York: New York Institute of Finance

Nison, Steve [1994]. *Beyond Candlesticks.* New York: John Wiley & Sons.

Williams, Michael S., and Amy Hoffman [2001]. *Fundamentals of the Options Market.* New York: McGraw-Hill.

Appendix B has a summary of most option strategies. Appendix C has the various expiration cycles.

Zelkin, Marvin H. [2002]. *It's Your Option: A Trader's Primer.* Greenville, SC: Traders Press, Inc.

CHAPTER SEVEN

LONG CALL CONDOR SPREADS

OVERVIEW OF A LONG CONDOR SPREAD

It may seem strange to start a discussion of option spreads with a calendar spread, a condor spread and a straddle (next chapter). There are two reasons for starting with these three option strategies. First, when a trader completely understands these strategies, the rest is easy. Second, these spreads offer the best setups for a switch spread.

The short call condor is a credit trade and offers no real opportunity for the switch version. The put version of the long condor is eliminated by screening criteria one in Chapter Three. This leaves the long call condor spread. A long call condor is constructed using four calls with consecutive strikes and the same expiration date. The lowest strike call is purchased. The two consecutive, middle strike calls are sold. The furthest out-of-the-money call is purchased. One of the two short calls is usually at-the-money. Maximum loss is limited to the debit required to put on the spread. Maximum profit is limited to the difference between the strikes minus the net debit. The expectation is that the underlying will trade in a range between the two inside calls. Although maximum profit occurs at expiration, when the underlying is trading between the two middle strikes, the long condor is profitable over a wider range. The downside breakeven point is the lowest strike plus the net debit. The upside breakeven point is the highest strike minus the net debit. Care should be taken to prevent commissions from eating the lion's share of the trading profit. One way of accomplishing this is to trade at least 10 contracts (one-thousand shares). The spread is always opened at a net debit.

Opening a condor spread one option position at a time, or legging into the spread, is dangerous. It could lead to an uncovered call position with all the attendant downside risks. In addition, legging into the spread will almost certainly result in a different-than-planned net debit. The result could be a spread with a net debit greater than the difference between the strikes. When this occurs, there is no winning combination. The spread is a guaranteed loss. It may sound improbable and, therefore, nothing to worry about. Please don't make that assumption. I did. It was very expensive. A trader friend of mine in Chicago asked me: "What did you do that *for*? I answered "*For* the last time!" Don't find yourself in this situation.

I prefer to use a long call condor when holding a long profitable position with enough stock to cover at least one of the short call positions — although I do not insist upon it. Holding enough stock to cover at least one of the short call positions increases the alternatives if some or all of the short calls are exercised. For example, delivering stock that has already been purchased can decrease commission costs by avoiding exercising one of the long call positions to fulfill an obligation created by an exercise notice. This would be a particularly attractive alternative when the trader is satisfied with the profit on the long stock. Holding a long stock position to cover one of the short calls has the added advantage of additional upside profit potential from the remaining long call. The long call condor is a versatile strategy that permits changes on-the-fly. For example, if the underlying breaks out up, profit can be increased beyond the theoretical maximum gain by closing the short calls and letting the long calls run. To illustrate, take XYZ stock trading at 20 with either a reversal or consolidation pattern. A long call condor could be constructed by purchasing a 17.5 and a 25 call and selling a 20 and 22.5 call. All four calls have the same expiration date. If the stock continues down the maximum loss is the net debit. If the underlying trades sideways, the spread is profitable. If the underlying reverses and breaks out in an uptrend, the short 20 and 22.5 calls can be closed by repurchasing at a loss which could be more than offset by the additional upside value of the long 17.5 and 22.5 calls. Agreed, the underlying might not be a good child and continue the uptrend. However, the condor is one of the few spreads that offer the possibility of reacting to the market and turning a loss into a potential gain that is greater than the original maximum possible gain. This is a particularly useful strategy with a switch long call condor and is discussed later in this chapter.

The long call condor is a relatively complex strategy. The maximum profit, the maximum loss and the breakeven points are not intuitively obvious. Therefore an explanation of how the long call condor works is necessary.

CALCULATING THE RELEVANT NUMBERS FOR A CONDOR SPREAD

Rather than using a theoretical example, the closing prices for Alcoa on January 16, 2004 are used to illustrate the calculations. The closing prices for Alcoa and the components of a long call option condor spread are provided below.

```
Date: January 16, 2004
Alcoa          35.04
Buy April 32.5 Call    (3.50)
Sell April 35 Call      2.15
Sell April 37.5 Call    1.15
Buy April 40 Call      (0.60)
     NET DEBIT              (0.80)
```

I have found it helpful to enter a positive value whenever there is cash in my account (an option is sold) and a negative number whenever there is cash out of my account (an option is purchased). This avoids the problem of deciding whether to add or subtract values. Simply add all the values algebraically. This is much easier and produces fewer calculation errors. Now let's consider the alternatives for the option condor spread when the spread is held until expiration.

Max Gain 1.70
Difference between
two consecutive strikes
minus the net debit

Maximum Gain Prices Between 35.00 and 37.50
Between either
of the two short Strikes

Maximum Loss (0.80)
Net Debit

Maximum Loss Prices 32.50 40.00
Either of the two
long strikes

Downside Breakeven Point 33.30
Low long call strike
plus net debit

Upside Breakeven Point 39.20
High long call strike
minus net debit

In the calculations below, values at expiration for the April 32.5 call and the April 40.00 call are positive because they would be sold to close the position and the sale would result in cash into the account. In like manner, values at expiration for the short April 35 call and the short April 37.5 call are negative because they would be purchased to close the position and the sale would result in cash flowing out of the account.

Why are the two short strikes the maximum profit points? Let's start with the April 35 strike and assume Alcoa closes at the lower short strike of 35.

Maximum Gain Lower Short Strike

Date: Expiration
Alcoa   35.00

option	open	value at expiration	gain/(loss)
April 32.5 Call	(3.50)	2.50	(1.00)
April 35 Call	2.15	0.00	2.15
April 37.5 Call	1.15	0.00	1.15
April 40 Call	(0.60)	0.00	(0.60)
		NET GAIN	1.70

When Alcoa closes at expiration at the highest short call strike of 37.5 the numbers are:

Maximum Gain Higher Short Strike

Date: Expiration

Alcoa   37.50

option	open	value at expiration	gain/(loss)
April 32.5 Call	(3.50)	5.00	1.50
April 35 Call	2.15	(2.50)	(0.35)
April 37.5 Call	1.15	0.00	1.15
April 40 Call	(0.60)	0.00	(0.60)
		NET GAIN	1.70

When the price closes below the lowest short strike (35.00), the value of the April 32.5 call is worth less than 2.50 and, therefore, the condor spread has a value less than 1.70. When Alcoa closes above the highest short strike (37.50), the short April 37.5 call has a value greater than 0.00 and results in a cash outflow to close. Therefore the condor spread has a value less than 1.70. Somebody out there will ask what happens when Alcoa closes between the two short strikes. Let's see.

Maximum Gain between the Short Strikes

Date: Expiration

Alcoa   36.25

option	open	value at expiration	gain/(loss)
April 32.5 Call	(3.50)	3.75	0.25
April 35 Call	2.15	(1.25)	0.90
April 37.5 Call	1.15	0.00	1.15
April 40 Call	(0.60)	0.00	(0.60)
		NET GAIN	1.70

The reason the gain or loss does not change when Alcoa closes between the two short middle strikes can be seen from the example. The additional gain on the long April 32.5 call (3.75 minus 2.50 or 1.25) is exactly offset by the loss (1.25) on the short April 35 call. This applies to any expiration price between the two short, middle strikes.

The maximum loss is equal to the net debit which occurs when the underlying closes at either of the two long strikes, in this case, when Alcoa closes at either 32.50 or 40.00. The calculations for these two strikes are given below.

Downside Maximum Loss at Lowest Strike

Date: Expiration

Alcoa   32.50

option	open	value at expiration	gain/(loss)
April 32.5 Call	(3.50)	0.00	(3.50)
April 35 Call	2.15	0.00	2.15
April 37.5 Call	1.15	0.00	1.15
April 40 Call	(0.60)	0.00	(0.60)
		NET LOSS	(0.80)

Upside Maximum Loss at Highest Strike

Date: Expiration

Alcoa   40.00

option	open	value at expiration	gain/(loss)
April 32.5 Call	(3.50)	7.50	4.00
April 35 Call	2.15	(5.00)	(2.85)
April 37.5 Call	1.15	(2.50)	(1.35)
April 40 Call	(0.60)	0.00	(0.60)
		NET LOSS	(0.80)

When Alcoa closes above 40.00, at expiration, any gains in the long calls are exactly offset by losses on the short calls. When Alcoa closes below 32.50 at expiration, all options expire worthless and the total loss remains equal to the original net debit.

The remaining calculations are the breakeven points. In this case there are two breakeven points rather than one. The lowest breakeven point is 33.30 or the lowest long call (32.50) plus the net debit (0.80). To verify this calculate the gain when Alcoa closes at 33.30 and 39.20.

Downside Breakeven Point

Date: Expiration

Alcoa closes at 32.50 plus 0.80 or **33.30**

option	open	value at expiration	gain/(loss)
April 32.5 Call	(3.50)	0.80	(2.70)
April 35 Call	2.15	0.00	2.15
April 37.5 Call	1.15	0.00	1.15
April 40 Call	(0.60)	0.00	(0.60)
		NET GAIN/LOSS	0.00

The highest breakeven point is 39.20 or the highest long call minus the net debit.

Upside Breakeven Point

Date: Expiration

Alcoa closes at 40.00 minus 0.80 or **39.20**

option	open	value at expiration	gain/(loss)
April 32.5 Call	(3.50)	6.70	3.20
April 35 Call	2.15	(4.20)	(2.05)
April 37.5 Call	1.15	(1.70)	(0.55)
April 40 Call	(0.60)	0.00	(0.60)
		NET GAIN/LOSS	0.00

Maximum gain, the maximum loss and the breakeven points at expiration are always calculated in this manner. The long call condor spread is the most complex and has been presented here.

SIMPLEST LONG CALL CONDOR USING OPTIONS

The simplest long call condor spread is opened for a net debit and all positions are closed at the same time. On February 9, 2004, Alcoa (AA) offered a good opportunity for the simplest long call condor. The relevant prices are provided below.

```
Underlying Stock:      34.94
    Buy April 32.5              (3.40)
    Sell April 35               1.80
    Sell April 37.5             0.90
    Buy April 40               (0.45)
               NET DEBIT            (1.15)


Maximum Gain:          1.35
Maximum Loss           1.15
Profitability Range:   33.65 to 38.85
```

The lower break even point is 33.65 or the lower strike of the lower purchased call plus the net debit. The higher breakeven point is 38.85 or the strike of the higher purchased call minus the net debit. This means the spread is profitable as long as the underlying closes between 33.65 and 38.85. The maximum gain is 1.35 or the net debit subtracted from the difference between two consecutive strikes. The maximum gain occurs when the underlying is between 35.00 and 37.50 at expiration.

I particularly like this long call condor setup for three reasons:
- The net debit is less than one-half of the difference between two consecutive strikes. This means the gain/loss ratio is greater than one.
- The spread is profitable over a relatively wide range.
- Implied volatility is lower than historical volatility of the underlying. The implied volatility of the four calls is 29.5, 28.0, 29.2 and 30.1 while the volatility of the underlying is 31.3. The immediately prior 20 days saw a historical volatility in the 35 percent range. This tends to confirm the viability of the spread. In general, the historical volatility trend and the implied volatility trend are better predictors of future volatility than a simple snapshot of historical and implied volatility.

The trade was closed on March 9 because the gain was 0.90 out of a maximum possible 1.35 and the underlying was trending downward and approaching 35.00 which is a maximum profit point. If the stock continues the downward trend, the profit could seriously suffer. As can be seen from Figure 7.1, the spread went from a profit to a loss by the time April expiration occurred. Another reason for closing the spread on March 9th is to capture some of the remaining time value in the long, two-strikes out-of-the-money April 40 call. It is often advisable to take a good gain rather than to get greedy and try for it all. A commonly quoted stock market adage is: The bulls get fat. The bears get fat. The pigs get eaten and the chickens get run over. The results from closing the spread on March 9th are provided below

April 32.5 Call	4.30	
April 35 Call	(1.80)	
April 37.5 Call	(0.75)	
April 40 Call	0.30	
Net Credit		2.05
Opening Net Debit		(1.15)
NET GAIN		0.90

FIGURE 7.1 provides a screen capture of this trade. The opening and closing days are indicated by the vertical dotted lines. The dotted horizontal lines on the underlying Alcoa stock chart represent the range of maximum profit between 35.00 and 37.50. The dashed horizontal lines represent the upper and lower break even points of 38.85 and 33.65. When the underlying closes outside of the dashed lines a loss occurs.

FIGURE 7.1: LONG CALL CONDOR SPREAD

The April calls were purchased rather than the March calls. The reason is simple. The net debit for the April long call condor was 1.15 while the net debit for the March long call condor was 1.35. How could this happen? All other things being equal, the net debit using the closer-in March calls should be less than the net debit using the longer-term April calls. The answer is provided by the implied volatility calculations. The implied volatilities for the March short calls are less than the implied volatilities of the short April calls and the implied volatilities of the long calls are about the same value. This means relatively less money is received from the sale of the two middle calls while the relative purchase price of the two outside calls remains about the same. This is an excellent example of the affect of implied volatility. Making a spread trade without calculating the implied volatiles can cost you money. The SG Option Calculator at *www.snowgold.com/download/downopt.html* is the one I prefer because it permits the use of different currencies, the ability to price options on futures, the calculation of implied volatilities, and a variety of graphical solutions. The SG Option Calculator also provides three option pricing alternatives: the Black-Scholes pricing model, the binomial pricing model and trinomial pricing model.

USING IMPLIED VOLATILITY CALCULATIONS TO EVALUATE AN OPTION CONDOR SPREAD

Assuming implied volatility remains constant, two things happen as the underlying increases in price: the delta of the lower, in-the-money, long call approaches 1.0 and the gamma of the out-of-the money, long call increases. Because of this, implied volatility and the value of the underlying are more important than time decay. The result is the selection criteria requiring short leg(s) of the spread with options that have between six and ten weeks to expiration does not apply to the long call condor spread. Experience shows a three to six-month out expiration date works quite well for the switch long call condor spread.

On January 16, 2004, Alcoa provided a good setup for a long call condor spread. Details of the option version of the condor spread are provided below.

Alcoa Close	35.04
Buy July 32.5 Call	(4.10)
Sell July 35 Call	2.95
Sell July 37.5 Call	1.85
Buy July 40 Call	(1.15)
NET DEBIT	(0.45)

Maximum Loss	0.45
Maximum Gain	2.05
Low Breakeven Point	32.95
High Breakeven Point	39.55

CALCULATING IMPLIED VOLATILITIES FOR MAXIMUM LOSS AND BREAKEVEN POINTS

The gain/loss ratio is an excellent 4.6 to 1.0. Other considerations are the breakeven points and the maximum loss points. It is always a good idea to calculate the implied volatility of the breakeven points and maximum loss points for all spreads. For the long call condor, it is absolutely essential. This can be done using any option calculator. For the low breakeven point, enter the difference between the current value of the underlying minus the lower breakeven point as the market price of an American style put option and calculate the implied volatility. For the high breakeven point, enter the difference between the high breakeven point minus the current value of the underlying as the market value of an American style call option and calculate the implied volatility. The result for the Alcoa example is an implied volatility of 0.351 for the low breakeven point and an implied volatility of 0.595 for the high breakeven point. The volatility required for the underlying to reach the low maximum loss point is 0.423. The volatility required for the underlying to reach the high maximum loss point is 0.654. Historical volatility of Alcoa was fluctuating in a narrow range around 0.35. Entering a condor spread without all of these volatility calculations is dangerous and could prove quite costly. The volatility calculations are summarized below.

Implied Volatilities of Critical Price Points for Option Condor Spread

Price	Implied Volatility
Low Maximum Loss 32.50	0.423
High Maximum Loss 40.00	0.654
Low Breakeven Point 32.95	0.351
High Breakeven Point 39.55	0.595

Volatility of Underlying: approximately 0.350

This is a very attractive option long call condor spread for three reasons:
- The initial cost is low, $450 for a spread on one thousand shares of stock.
- The gain/loss ratio is high, 4.6 to 1.0.
- Based on the implied volatilities of the critical price points, there is a high probability of taking enough profit from the trade to cover commissions plus enough of a gain to make the trade worthwhile.

The simplest long call condor spread closes all open positions at the same time. When the outlook includes a slightly bullish dimension, another alternative is to close all open positions except the long, out-of-the-money call. When this can be done on a breakeven or better basis, the net result is a free long call option. If the underlying continues to increase, the result is additional gains. This must be done carefully. Be sure to include transaction costs when calculating the breakeven point. The risk is that the underlying will either trade sideways or decrease in value. When this happens, commissions could eat up any gains. An example of this strategy is provided in the next section.

OPTION CONDOR SPREAD

This strategy is best used with three to six month options because there is enough time for the long, out-of-the-money call option to yield a gain. Bristol-Myers, Squibb (BMY) presented such a setup on April 4, 2004.

<u>Option Long Call Condor Spread Closing Long Highest Call Last</u>

	Opening data		Close 1 Data		Close 2 Data	
Date:	04/04/03		05/20/03		6/17/04	
BMY Close:	22.50		23.50		28.86	
Buy June 20	(3.10)	Sell June 20 Call	3.50			
Sell June 22.5 Call	1.50	Buy June 22.5 Call	(1.40)			
Sell June 25 Call	0.50	Buy June 25 Call	(0.40)			
Buy June 27.5 Call	(0.10)	Leave Open	___	Sell June 27.5 Call	1.55	
Net Credit/(Debit)	(1.20)		1.70		1.55	
Cumulative Net Gain/(Loss)			**0.50**		**2.05**	

If each part of the condor spread contains 10 contracts, the original net debit is $1,200 and the net gain from Close One is $500. This provides ample room to cover transaction costs plus a small profit. The long out-of-the-money call only cost 0.10; therefore, even a risk averse trader would probably not close the deep in-the-money long call at this point. When the long June 22.75 call is closed for 1.55 three days before expiration on June 17th, the result is an additional $1,550 for a total trading gain, before commissions, of $2,050. This is a nice return. A trader willing to accept more risk will leave both long calls open when a break out to the upside is a possibility.

<u>Closing Both Long Positions Last</u>

To realize a profit and to eliminate the possibility of being exercised, the short calls are closed at a slight profit, usually at least enough to cover commissions. When this strategy is used, a stop on the in-the-money option that is contingent on the price of the underlying is needed to protect some of the profit. An example of this strategy would be to close the short BMY 22.5 call and the short BMY June 25 calls and leave the long June 20 and June 27.5 calls open. The results of this strategy are provided below.

	Opening data		Close 1 Data		Close 2 Data	
Date:	04/04/03		05/20/03		6/17/04	
BMY Close:	22.50		23.50		28.86	
Buy June 20	(3.10)	Leave Open		Sell June 20 Call	8.10	
Sell June 22.5 Call	1.50	Buy June 22.5 Call	(1.40)			
Sell June 25 Call	0.50	Buy June 25 Call	(0.40)			
Buy June 27.5 Call	(0.10)	Leave Open	___	Sell June 27.5 Call	1.55	
Net Credit/(Debit)	(1.20)		(1.80)		9.65	
		NET GAIN	0.20		6.45	
		Cumulative Net Gain			**6.65**	

There is additional risk when closing a long condor spread this way. The net debit to open the spread is 1.20 and the net debit to close the two short options is 1.80. This makes a total net debit of 3.00. However, the intrinsic value of the long June 20 call is 3.50 so, on paper, the position is 0.50 or $500 in-the-money. Care should be taken to prevent the position from going from a profit to a loss. This is done by placing a trailing protective stop.

The cumulative net gain from leaving both long positions open is quite good. However, the switch version offers more flexibility and a better return. As always, the additional downside risk from the long single stock future must be managed with effective protective stops.

SWITCH CONDOR SPREAD

A good switch call condor spread set up meets the following criteria:

- The outlook is neutral to slightly bullish.
- The underlying is trading close to a strike price.
- The net credit is close to the difference between two consecutive strikes.

These are relevant because, with a long single stock future and three calls, there is no real downside protection. The BMY switch long call condor that is equivalent to the option long call condor is constructed by buying the BMY single stock future when the underlying is selling at 22.50, selling the June 22.5 call, selling the June 25 call and buying the far out-of-the-money June 27.5 call. When the net credit on the option part of the switch trade is close to the difference between two consecutive strikes, the breakeven point of the single stock future is close to the long lower strike of the option spread (in this case 20.00). The affect of this is the equivalent of receiving the long, lower priced option for free. To provide a benchmark, the switch condor is closed in the same manner as the option condor spread. The relevant prices using the single stock future (SSF) are provided below.

Switch Long Call Condor Spread Closing Long Highest Call Last

	Opening data		Close 1 Data		Close 2 Data	
Date:	04/04/03		05/20/03		6/17/04	
BMY Close:	22.50		23.50		28.86	
Buy BMY June SSF	(22.28)	Sell June SSF	23.26			
Sell June 22.5 Call	1.50	Buy June 22.5 Call	(1.40)			
Sell June 25 Call	0.50	Buy June 25 Call	(0.40)			
Buy June 27.5 Call	(0.10)	Leave Open	____	Sell June 27.5 Call	1.55	
Net Credit/(Debit)	(20.38)		21.46		1.55	
		Cumulative Gain	**1.08**		**2.63**	

Notice two differences between the switch version and the option version:

1. The switch condor spread has a gain on Close 1 of 1.08 versus 0.50 for the option long call condor spread.
2. The switch long call condor has a 28.3 percent greater net gain than the option long call condor spread (2.63 vs. 2.05.)

Difference One means, at Close 1, the switch spread has a guaranteed initial gain that is 116 percent greater than the option spread. The 1.08 gain translates to $1,080 for one thousand shares. This is certainly enough to cover any transaction costs and still leave a nice gain on the spread. Closing the short calls when analysis indicates the possibility of a break out up, has the added advantage of eliminating the possibility of having to meet a call for the stock. The long single stock future can be left open when technical analysis indicates the probability of a strong uptrend. When this strategy is used, be sure to use a tight stop on the long single stock future to protect against the potential unlimited downside risk. A high risk averse trader would always close the long single stock future rather than leave it open. A moderate risk trader will close the single stock future when either a reversal point or a target price is reached before the expiration date of the options used for the spread. An example of this strategy would be to close both the short BMY June 22.5 call and the short June 25 call and leave both the long September single stock future (SSF) and the long BMY June 27.5 call open. The results of this strategy are provided below.

<u>Switch Long Call Condor Spread Closing Both Long Positions Last</u>

	Opening data		Close 1 Data		Close 2 Data	
Date:	04/04/03		05/20/03		6/17/04	
BMY Close:	22.50		23.50		28.86	
Buy BMY Sep SSF	(22.28)		Leave Open		Sell Sep SSF	28.66
Sell June 22.5 Call	1.50	Buy June 22.5 Call	(1.40)		
Sell June 25 Call	0.50	Buy June 25 Call	(0.40)		
Buy June 27.5 Call	(0.10)	Leave Open	_____	Sell June 27.5 Call	1.55
Net Credit/(Debit)	(20.38)		(1.80)		30.21
		Trading Net Gain	0.20		
Effective Net Credit	2.12	Position Status	1.32	**NET GAIN**	**8.03**

The Effective Net Credit (2.12) is the BMY close (22.50) minus the cost of the BMY single stock future (22.28) plus the amount received for the two short option positions (2.00) minus the price of the long out-of-the-money 27.50 call (0.10). The Trading Net Gain at Close One is 0.20 or the difference between the amounts received for the two short options (2.00) and the amount paid to close the two short options at Close One (1.80). The Position Status at Close One (1.32) is the result of three calculations. The first calculation is the single stock future gain which is equal to the price of BMY (23.50) minus the price of BMY when the position was opened (22.50) (The cost of the single stock future is not used because it has already been factored into the effective net credit.) The second calculation is the addition of the original net credit (2.12) to the gain from the single stock future. Finally, the debit incurred by closing the two short calls (1.80) is subtracted from the total of calculation two. The value of the long out-of-the-money call is not used in the calculations at Close One because the only value attributable to the long out-of-the-money call option is its time value. The long out-of-the-money call has no intrinsic value.

Part of the 1.32 gain in position status at Close One must be protected by a trailing stop. When there is no logical price for a trailing protective stop, close the long single stock future. The NET GAIN is equal to the algebraic sum of the Net Credit/(Debit) row. Although the final net gain is three times greater than closing the single stock future when the short options are closed, this strategy has more risk because less profit is taken when only the short calls are closed. This is the reason the strategy of closing both long positions after closing both short positions should only be used by experienced traders who are willing to accept a higher level of risk. A September single stock future, rather than a June single stock future, is used to provide another opportunity for any type of spread that uses a long single stock future position. The reason this works is there is no significant difference between the cost of a September single stock future and a June single stock future because time and implied volatility are not part of the price of a single stock future. This has two advantages. First, the next switch spread can be opened at lower transaction costs because there is no cost to open the long lower position – it is already open. Second, the gain from the long single stock future can be used to margin future transactions.

Closing both long positions last is a viable trade only with a switch spread and should be used only by traders who are willing to accept higher levels of risk.

CONCLUSION

The long call condor is, arguably, the most complex and versatile spread. It consists of four calls with consecutive strikes. The lowest and highest calls are purchased and the two middle calls are sold short. The switch long call condor uses a single stock future to replace the lowest long call. Although maximum profit occurs at expiration when the underlying is trading between the two middle strikes, the long condor is profitable over a wider range. The downside breakeven point is the lowest strike plus the net debit. The upside breakeven point is the highest strike minus the net debit. The option condor spread is always opened at a net debit.

All four positions of an option condor spread should be opened at the same time for a specified net debit. For the switch version, the single stock future is used to replace the low, long call and should be opened first to avoid an uncovered call position. The three option positions should be opened together for a specified net credit. When the three calls cannot by opened shortly after opening a long single stock future position, consider closing the long single stock future and avoiding the spread. **Care should be taken to prevent commissions from eating the lion's share of the trading profit.** One way of accomplishing this is to trade at least 10 contracts (one-thousand shares).

REFERENCES

Allure, Marc [2003]. *The Option Strategist.* New York: McGraw-Hill.

Fontanills, George A [1998]. *The Options Course.* New York: John Wiley & Sons.
> Excellent introduction to options. Clearly written in small, easy-to-learn steps.

Fontanills, George A. [1998]. *The Options Course Workbook: Step-By-Step Exercises and Tests to Help You Master the Options Course.* New York: John Wiley & Sons.
> The title says it all. An excellent workbook that teaches how to apply the concepts in the companion text.

Fontanills, George and Tom Gentile [2003]. *The Volatility Course.* New York: John Wiley & Sons.
> Emphasizes volatility as a market tool. Examines and explains every aspect of volatility and the importance of volatility to option trading. Provides trading strategies under a variety of situations. Covers how to quantify volatility strategies based on volatility and strategies for high and low volatility markets.

Gallacher, William R. [1999]. *The Options Edge.* New York: McGraw-Hill.
> A book for intermediate and above option traders that want to eliminate all the complexity surrounding option analysis and trading.

McMillan, Lawrence G. [2002]. *Options as a Strategic Investment. 4th Edition.* ew York: New York Institute of Finance.

McMillan, Lawrence G. [2002]. *Profit with Options.* New York: John Wiley & Sons.

McMillan, Lawrence G. [1996]. *McMillan on Options.* New York: John Wiley & Sons.

Options Institute, The (Ed.) [1999]. *Options: Essential Concepts & Trading Strategies 3rd Edition.* New York: McGraw-Hill.

How market makers trade. pp. 253-273. The predictive power of options. pp. 357-388.

Trester, Kenneth R. [2002]. *The Complete Options Player 4th Edition.* Lake Tahoe, NY: Institute for Options Research.

Williams, Michael S., and Amy Hoffman [2001]. *Fundamentals of the Options Market.* New York: McGraw-Hill.

Appendix A has a summary of order types. Appendix B has a summary of most option strategies. Appendix C has the various expiration cycles.

Zelkin, Marvin H. [2002]. *It's Your Option: A Trader's Primer.* Greenville, SC: Traders Press, Inc.

CHAPTER EIGHT

THE STRADDLE

OVERVIEW OF STRADDLES

A straddle is the purchase (or sale) of a call and a put with the same strike and expiration date. Because the screening criteria for switch spreads exclude short puts, only a long straddle or the purchase of a put and call is considered. Long straddles are normally placed when the historical volatility is at a cyclical low. The expectation is for an increase in volatility with the direction of the price move uncertain. If the underlying increases in value beyond the cost of the straddle, the trader makes a profit from the call part of the straddle. If the stock decreases in value beyond the cost of the straddle, the trader makes a profit from the put part of the straddle. If the stock trades sideways, the trader loses money because of time decay. The maximum loss is the cost of the initial debit which occurs when the underlying closes at the strike price on expiration. Occasionally, but not often, a profit is made on both parts of a straddle.

The problem with placing profitable straddles is a stock with low cyclical historical volatility often has options with high implied volatilities. This is because everyone can see the stock has a low volatility and they are expecting an increase in volatility. Therefore, a trader who goes long a straddle is paying for the expected increase in volatility twice:
- a high premium for the implied volatility of the call and
- a high premium for the implied volatility of the put.

Replacing one of the options with a single stock future eliminates the high premium paid for one of the options because the price of a single stock future is not related to volatility. Unlike most switch spreads, the single stock future portion of the switch straddle does not have unlimited loss potential. When a long single stock future is switched for the long call, maximum loss is limited to the insurance provided by the long put plus the cost of the long put.

Three switch straddle opportunities are provided using American International Group (AIG):
- Switch Straddle Using Long Single Stock Future and Options with High Implied Volatilities.
- Switch Straddle Using Short Single Stock Future and Options with High Implied Volatilities.
- Switch Straddle Using Long Single Stock Future with Low Volatility Stock and Low Volatility Options.

SWITCH STRADDLE USING LONG SINGLE STOCK FUTURE AND OPTIONS
WITH HIGH IMPLIED VOLATILITIES

The setup is provided by the AIG daily chart in **FIGURE 8.1**. The thick solid line at the top (see arrow) represents strong, long-term crossover support to resistance which was formed before the beginning of the daily chart. This line was drawn based on a long-term weekly chart. The top of the first down gap is represented by the dashed line. Solid lines indicate the tops and bottoms of long black bodies. Dotted lines represent the midpoints of long black bodies. The rectangle in the lower right-hand corner identifies a candlestick pattern called an unconfirmed morning star. Somebody out there will notice the bottom two solid lines and the bottom dotted line are not drawn based on a long black body. This is because three consecutive down black bodies are considered as one, long, three-day black body. Combining candles in this manner prevents cluttering the chart with lines and also increases the robustness of the analysis.

FIGURE 8.1: AIG STRADDLE SETUP

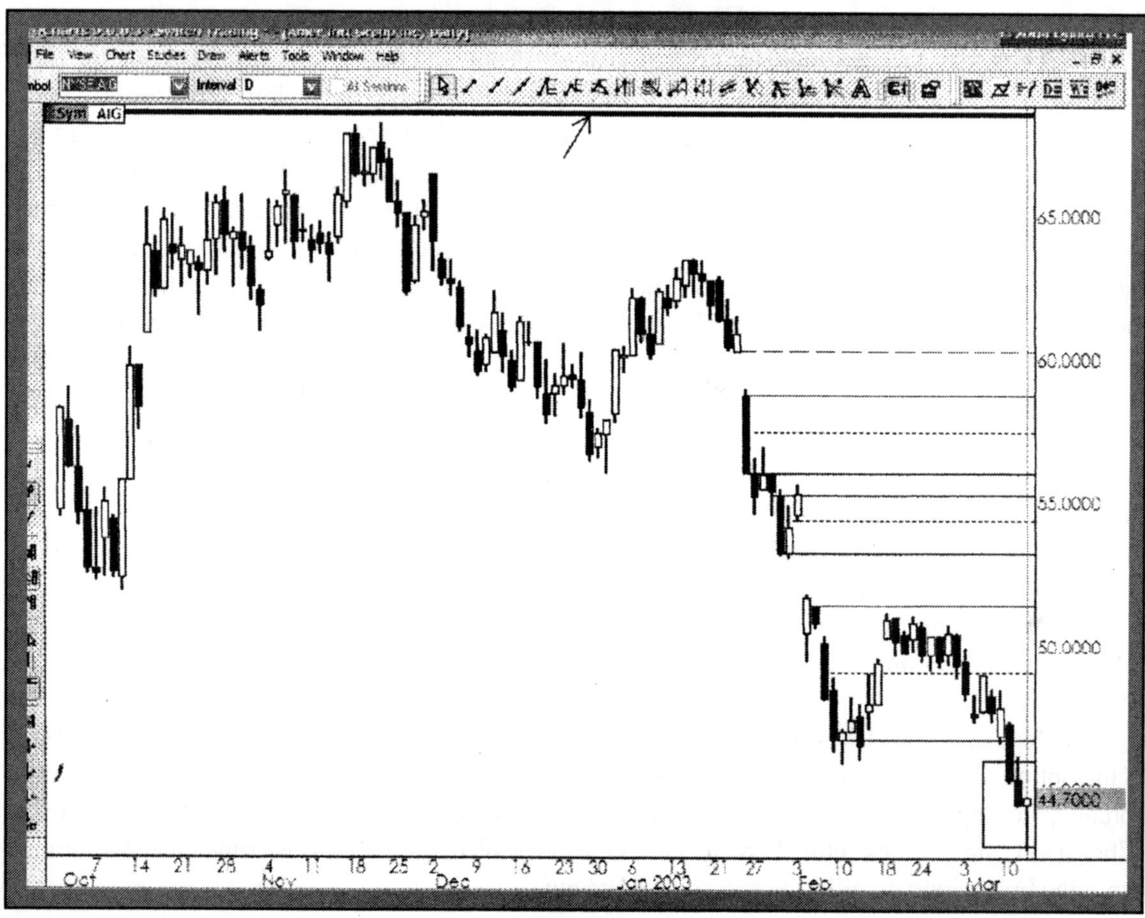

The Doji morning star on March 12, 2003 represents an excellent place for a straddle. The expectation is for a reversal up. If this occurs the long call could become profitable. However the morning star has not been confirmed on March 12th. As a result, there is a chance that the downtrend could continue. If this happens, the long put could become profitable. The expectation is that AIG will probably move in one direction or the other.

This expectation is reflected by the relatively high implied volatilities of the short-term May 45 Call and Put.

Volatilities

AIG (Historical 20-Day)	0.380
May 45 Put (Implied)	0.532
May 45 Call (Implied)	0.403

Long straddles with high volatility options are seldom profitable. The underlying has to move too far to cover the cost of high premiums on both the call and put. On March 12, 2003, American International Group (AIG) offered such a situation.

- Option Debit Straddle

Buy May 45 Call	(3.00)
Buy May 45 Put	(3.90)
Option Straddle Net Debit	(6.90)

The difference between the call implied volatility of 0.403 and the AIG volatility at 0.380 might seem too small to be a factor. However, this makes a difference of 0.17 per share or $170 on one-thousand shares which translates to five percent of the price of the market price of the May 45 call.

When the underlying goes up, the breakeven point for the option straddle is calculated by adding the net debit to the strike price. When the underlying goes down, the breakeven point is the net debit subtracted from the strike price. The maximum loss of the option straddle is the net debit of 6.90

Breakeven Points for Option Straddle

Strike	45.00	
plus Net Debit	6.90	
Option Straddle Upside BEP		51.90
Strike	45.00	
minus Net Debit	6.90	
Option Straddle Downside BEP		38.10

The option straddle zone of loss ranges from 38.10 to 51.90. The switch straddle offers a more attractive alternative.

- Equivalent Switch Straddle

Buy Single Stock Future	44.75	
AIG Close	44.70	
Single Stock Future "Premium"		(0.05)
Buy May 45 Put		(3.90)
Switch Straddle Net Debit		(3.95)

When the underlying increases in value, the breakeven point for the switch long straddle is calculated by adding the net debit to the cost of the long single stock future.

Breakeven Point Up for the Long Switch Straddle
    Cost of AIG Single Stock Future   44.70
    plus Net Debit   3.95
        Single Stock Future Upside BEP   48.65

The long switch straddle breakeven point to the upside is 48.65 while the option straddle BEP is 51.90. So far so good. However, there is a downside. If AIG goes down, the long switch straddle could lose money unless the long single stock future position is closed. The maximum loss of the switch straddle with a long single stock future occurs when the underlying decreases in value. For the current example the maximum possible loss is 3.65 This calculation does not include transaction costs and assumes the trader exercises the May 45 put by first exercising the long single stock future to obtain the necessary stock. The calculations are provided below.

Maximum Loss of Long Switch Straddle
    Strike Of May 45 Put   45.00
    minus Cost of Long Single Stock Future   (44.75)
        Gain from Put Exercise   0.25
        Cost Of Long Put   (3.90)
            Maximum Loss of Long Switch Straddle   3.65

The 3.65 maximum loss for the long switch straddle assumes all positions are held to the expiration of the long put. This maximum loss changes when the long single stock future is closed before the long put in order to provide a downside profit.

The breakeven point down for the option straddle is the strike price minus the net debit. The option straddle begins making money when AIG falls below 38.10.

Option Straddle Breakeven Point Down
    Strike   45.00
    minus Net Debit   6.90
        Option Straddle Downside BEP   38.10

When the AIG goes down there is good news and there is bad news for the long switch straddle. The good news is there is a limited loss that is equal to 3.65. The bad news is when the cost of the single stock future is below the strike of the put, the long switch straddle will never make money unless the long single stock future is closed. The reason is any gain from the long put will be offset by the losses of the long single stock future. This means the long switch straddle needs an initial protective stop on the downside. A good price for the initial protective stop is the strike of the long put minus one-half of the difference between the net debit for the option straddle and the net debit for the long switch straddle. The rationale is when the underlying continues down and the downside protective stop is placed at this price, the gain from the long switch straddle is always greater than the gain from the option straddle.

There are two parts to the downside breakeven point.
First calculate the initial downside protective stop.
Initial Protective Stop Calculations

Strike of Long Put		45.00
Minus		
Option Straddle Net Debit	6.90	
minus		
Long Switch Straddle Net Debit	<u>3.95</u>	
	2.95	
Divided by 2 and subtract		(1.48)
Downside Initial Protective Stop		43.52

Second, subtract the long switch net debit from the initial protective stop.
Downside Breakeven Point for Long Switch Straddle

Initial Protective Stop	43.52
minus Long Switch Net Debit	(3.95)
Downside Breakeven Point for Long Switch Straddle	39.57

Placing the initial protective stop at this point means the breakeven point for the switch straddle is 39.57 and the breakeven point for the option straddle is 38.10. As a result, when the option straddle is at the breakeven point, the switch straddle is 1.47 in the money. Therefore, using this strategy means the switch straddle will always yield 1.47 more on the downside. When the initial protective stop is too close to the price of the underlying, avoid this trade.

Although the percentage moves needed and the implied volatilities seem high, let us assume for a moment that the option straddle was opened on March 12, 2003. The time to close the straddle is on April 23, 2003 when AIG approaches the bottom of the top down gap which is also the top of the long black body. **FIGURE 8.2** provides a screen capture of the life of the straddle. In passing it might be noted that it is always a good idea to take a screen capture summarizing every trade. Figure 8.2 contains daily charts for the May 45 put, the May 45 call and underlying AIG stock. The entry bars are the solid vertical lines. The vertical dotted lines pass through the exit point on April 23, 2003. Traders familiar with Fibonacci and Elliott Wave analyses will recognize some obvious patterns and turning points.

FIGURE 8.2: AIG STRADDLE HISTORY

The results of exiting the AIG May 45 option straddle on April 23, 2003 are given below.

- May 45 Call

Buy On March 12, 2003	(3.00)
Sell On April 23, 2003	13.20
Net Gain from Call	10.20

- May 45 Put

Buy On March 12, 2003	(3.90)
Sell On April 23, 2003	0.05
Net Loss from Put	(3.85)
Gain from Option Straddle	6.35

In practice the long May 45 put would have been left open. The actual reward/risk ratio is the result of a particular trade as opposed to the theoretical reward/risk ratio of a position before it is opened. This is a useful statistic for positions, such as a long straddle, with unlimited potential gains. The maximum risk for a long straddle is the initial net debit. Therefore, the net gain on the straddle is 6.35 on a maximum risk of 6.90. This represents an actual reward/risk ratio of 0.92. This is not a good return because the large move required by the underlying makes this a relatively risky trade. The equivalent switch straddle offers a situation where the stock does not have to move quite so far. The mechanics of the equivalent switch straddle trade are provided below.

- AIG Single Stock Future
  Buy On March 12, 2003   (44.75)
  Sell On April 23, 2003   58.31
     Net Gain from Single Stock Future 13.56
- May 45 Put
  Buy On March 12, 2003   (3.90)
  Sell On April 23, 2003   0.05
        Net Loss from Put   (3.85)
Gain from Switch Straddle with Long Future   9.71

The maximum loss from the option straddle is equal to the net debit of 6.90. The maximum loss of the switch straddle is 3.65 which is the insurance provided by the long May 45 put plus the cost of the May 45 put. The actual reward/risk ratio for the switch spread is 2.7. The 9.75 net gain from the switch straddle is 53.5 percent higher than 6.35 net gain from the option straddle. The put was closed to provide a benchmark. In practice the long put would have been left open with the hope of an AIG price reversal which would make the put profitable.

SWITCH STRADDLE USING SHORT SINGLE STOCK FUTURE AND OPTIONS WITH HIGH IMPLIED VOLATILITIES

Another way to construct this trade would have been to go short the single stock future and long the call. Purchasing the May 45 call and selling the single stock future short results in a net debit of 2.95.

Switch Straddle with Short Single Stock Future
        Sell Single Stock Future   44.75
        AIG Close   44.70
        Single Stock Future "Premium"   0.05
        Buy May 45 Call   (3.00)
Switch Straddle Net Debit   (2.95)

Purchasing the lower priced call and switching a short single stock future for the higher priced put decreases the net debit by 1.00 so this would be the trade of choice if the trader is truly neutral about the direction of the move. As in the case of the long single stock future, the risk due to the short single stock future is not unlimited. If the position moves against you, part of the loss from the short single stock future is insured by the long May 45 call.

Maximum Risk
        Short AIG Single Stock Future   44.75
        Strike of May 45 call   (45.00)
        Net Loss from Exercising May 45 call   (0.25)
        Cost of Long May 45 call   (3.00)
                Maximum Loss   (3.25)

This straddle should be placed by first opening the long May 45 call and then shorting the single stock future. This is possible because the single stock future can be shorted on a down tick. The initial protective stop for the short single stock future should be triggered if the morning star pattern is confirmed. The long white, up gap bar the day after the entry bar is a rising window that provides confirmation of the Doji morning star (Figure 8.2). It cost 47.80 to repurchase the short single stock future. The results of the switch straddle with a short single stock future are provided below.

- AIG Single Stock Future
  Buy On March 12, 2003   44.75
  Sell On April 23, 2003   (47.80)
  Net Loss from Single Stock Future   (3.05)
- May 45 Call
  Buy On March 12, 2003   (3.00)
  Sell On April 23, 2003   13.20
        Net Gain from Call   10.20
  Gain from Switch Straddle with Short Future   7.15

The short single stock future switch alternative did not perform as well as the long single stock future alternative because AIG reversed to an uptrend rather than continuing the downtrend. This illustrates a point that most option traders already know. The basis for selecting between two options should not be made on the basis of the price of the two options. In the case of a switch straddle with the long single stock future, the choice is made based on the directional bias of the trader. A straddle using high volatility options has been presented. The switch straddle also works with low volatility options.

SWITCH STRADDLE USING LONG SINGLE STOCK FUTURE WITH LOW VOLATILITY STOCK AND LOW VOLATILITY OPTIONS

On October 27, 2003 AIG presented an excellent opportunity to open a long switch straddle. Historical volatility was at a twenty-one month low. The December 60 put and call also had low implied volatilities.

- Volatilities
  AIG (Historical 20-Day)   0.180
  December 60 Call (Implied)   0.218
  December 60 Put (Implied)   0.263

The long option and switch straddle mechanics are provided below.

- Option Debit Straddle

    Buy December 60 Call   (2.15)

    Buy December 60 Put   (2.25)

      Option Straddle Net Debit (4.40)

- Equivalent Switch Straddle

    Buy December Single Stock Future (59.96)

    AIG Close   59.98

      Single Stock Future "Premium" 0.02

    Buy December 60 Put   (2.25)

      Switch Straddle Net Debit (2.23)

In this case the straddle is closed one leg at a time. The long put is closed on November 21, 2003 while the long call is held until the day before expiration, December 18, 2003. The results of exiting the option straddle using this strategy are given below.

- December 60 Put

    Buy On October 27, 2003 (2.25)

    Sell On November 21, 2003 3.80

      Net Gain from Put 1.55

- December 60 Call

    Buy On October 27, 2003 (2.15)

    Sell On December 17, 2003 4.00

      Net Gain from Call 1.85

       Gain from Option Straddle 3.40

Straddles are closed one leg at a time when the trader thinks the stock is about to reverse directions. The advantage of closing one leg at a time is decreased risk. Once the put has been closed for a profit at 1.55, the maximum loss is lowered form 4.40 to 2.85 (4.40 minus 1.55). This is always a judgment call. However, straddles are often closed this way when a stock is bouncing back and forth between two clearly defined price levels.

The results from closing the switch straddle in the same manner as the option straddle are provided below.

- May 45 Put

    Buy On October 27, 2003 (2.25)

    Sell On November 21, 2003 3.80

      Net Gain from Put 1.55

- AIG December Single Stock Future

    Buy On October 27, 2003 (59.96)

    Sell On December 17, 2003 64.09

    Net Gain from Single Stock Future 4.13

       Gain from Switch Straddle 5.68

The gain from the switch straddle is 5.68 compared to a 3.40 gain from the option straddle. This represents an improvement of sixty-seven percent.

CONCLUSION

Three straddle opportunities were provided using American International Group (AIG):

- A switch straddle using a long single stock future and options with high implied volatilities.
- A switch straddle using a short single stock future and options with high implied volatilities.
- A switch straddle using a long single stock future with a low volatility stock and low volatility options.

Two versions of a switch straddle were provided for a straddle with high volatility options: a switch straddle with a long single stock future and a long put and a switch straddle with a long call and a short single stock future. Both legs of these straddles were closed at the same time. The second example using low volatilities closed one leg at a time. It was also pointed out that, unlike most switch spreads, the single stock future portion of the switch straddle does not have unlimited loss potential. The long single stock future that is switched for the long call has a loss limited to the insurance provided by the long put plus the cost of the long put. The short single stock future that is switched for the long put has a loss potential that is insured by the long call plus the cost of the long call.

REFERENCES

Allure, Marc [2003]. *The Option Strategist.* New York: McGraw-Hill.

Angell, George. [1983]. *Sure Thing Options Trading.* New York: Plume (Penguin Group.

McMillan, Lawrence G. [2002]. *Options as a Strategic Investment. 4th Edition.* New York: New York Institute of Finance.

McMillan, Lawrence G. [2002]. *Profit with Options.* New York: John Wiley & Sons.

Nison, Steve [2001]. *Japanese Candlestick Charting Techniques 2nd Edition.* New York: New York Institute of Finance

Nison, Steve [1994]. *Beyond Candlesticks.* New York: John Wiley & Sons.

Williams, Michael S., and Amy Hoffman [2001]. *Fundamentals of the Options Market.* New York: McGraw-Hill.
    Appendix A has a summary of order types. Appendix B has a summary of most option strategies. Appendix C has the various expiration cycles.

Zelkin, Marvin H. [2002]. *It's Your Option: A Trader's Primer.* Greenville, SC: Traders Press, Inc.

CHAPTER NINE

VERTICAL CALL DEBIT SPREAD

OVERVIEW OF VERTICAL CALL DEBIT SPREAD

A vertical call debit spread, also called a call bull debit spread, is used when a trader has a slightly bullish outlook on a stock. It involves the purchase of one call with a certain strike and the sale of another call at a higher strike. Both options must be on the same underlying stock and have the same expiration date. The lower price long call always costs more than the higher priced short call. Therefore, the spread always results in a debit. The equivalent switch spread uses the short out-of-the-money call and replaces the long at-the-money or in-the-money call with a long single stock futures contract. Several examples of this spread were used in Chapter Two and Chapter Three.

This is a versatile strategy with many uses. Futures traders could use it as an alternative to "matched pairs" trading where matched pairs trading is considered inappropriate because of statistical considerations. Option traders can use the switch bull call spread to improve the profit potential of a traditional call bull spread. Even long-term stock investors, who do not want to run the risk of having their stock called away, might find the switch bull call spread useful. In certain situations, this spread could permit long-term stock investors to average up at a cost below the current stock price. How and why does the switch bull call spread work?

The vertical call debit spread works because the long call option always has a higher delta than the short call option. Delta is a measure of the amount an option price changes when the underlying stock price changes by one dollar. The more an option is in-the-money the higher the delta.

Although the Profit/Loss graph for a switch bull call spread is identical to a covered write, the two strategies have different objectives and position management considerations. The primary objective of covered call writing, for most investors, is increased income through stock ownership. The primary objective of the switch bull call spread does not usually include stock ownership. The primary objective of the switch bull spread is to increase the profit potential of a traditional vertical call debit spread. The switch bull spread involves replacing the long, lower strike call with a single stock future and then shorting the next higher strike call option, in that order. A long single stock future is switched for the long call option, thereby, switching a traditional debit position into a credit position. Position management differences are significant and are covered in the Position Management Considerations section of this chapter.

On September 8, 2003, Emulex Corp. (ELX) offered a good opportunity for a vertical call debit spread. Normally the short call is one strike higher than the long call. However, when the increase in potential gain is large enough to justify the increased debit, the short call is placed two strikes away from the long call. This type of setup occurred on August 6, 2003.

FIGURE 9.1: ELX VERTICAL CALL DEBIT SPREAD SETUP

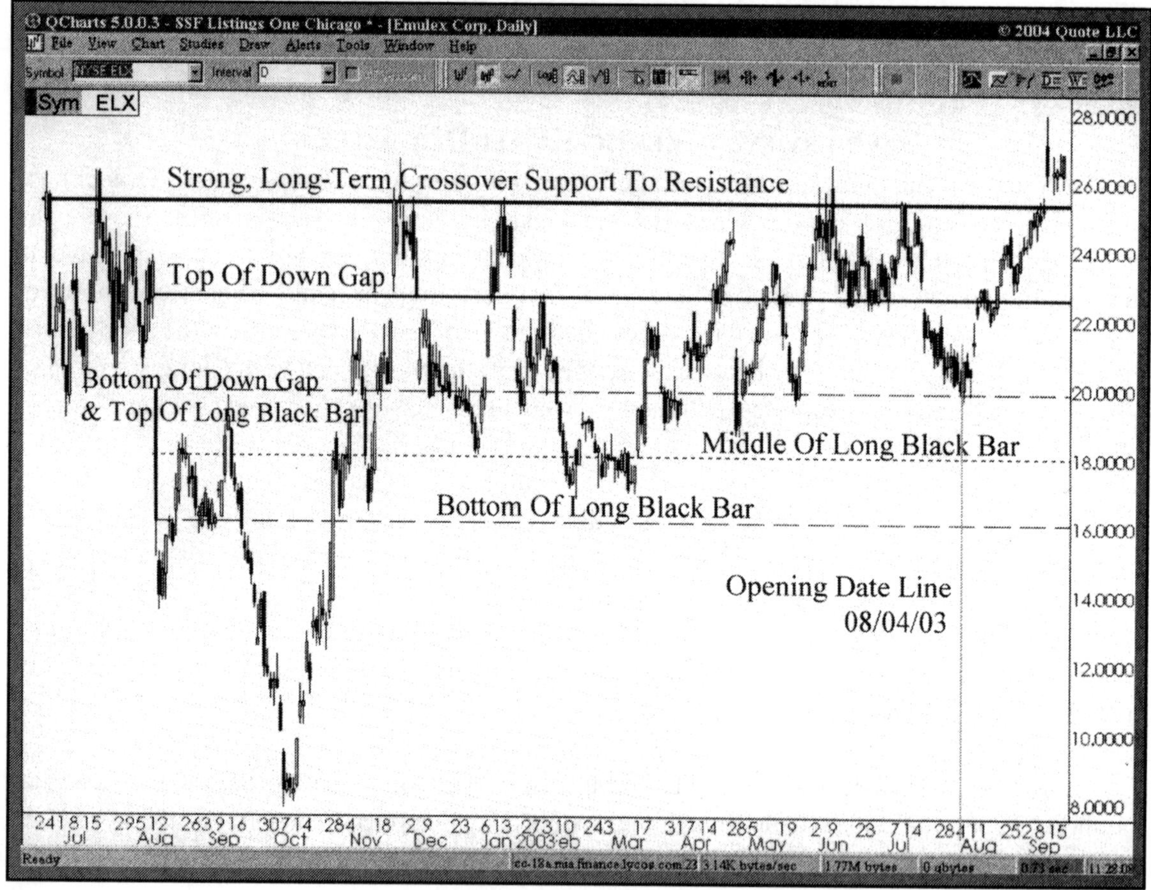

Strong, long-term crossover support to resistance occurred about 25.50. ELX quickly went from about 20.00 to 8.00. After a quick recovery, ELX settled into a trading range between the middle of a long black bar at 18.00 and crossover from support to resistance at 25.50. In April of 2003 the trading range narrowed to the bottom of the down gap and the top of a long black bar at 20.00. Once a clear trading area was established (between 20.00 and 25.50), a good entry point for a vertical call debit spread would be a clear reversal signal on a brief down turn from the crossover support to resistance line at 25.50 down to the bottom of the down gap and the top of a long black body at 20.00. This situation occurred on August 4, 2003. Because ELX is expected to recover to 25.50 and then reverse direction, the two strikes should be 20.00 and 25.00. There is a 22.50 strike between these strikes, however, the risk of being called away from a profitable spread is considered too great to use this strike. The position should be closed if ELX clearly breaks the expected resistance level of 25.50 or if the short call reaches parity. Parity is the value at which the strike plus the premium is less than or equal to the price of the underlying. The lower strike should be slightly in-the-money to increase the credit from the short call. If support at 20.00 fails, a drop to the next support level at 18.00 can be expected. If support fails at this level a drop to 16.00 is quite possible. Therefore, from a technical analysis viewpoint, reasonable places for an initial protective stop would be at 20.00 or slightly above 18.00. The exact placement of the initial protective stop is discussed in the position management section.

OPTION VERTICAL CALL DEBIT SPREAD COMPARED TO SWITCH VERTICAL CALL DEBIT SPREAD

The mechanics of opening the option spread are illustrated using the closing prices for ELX on August 6, 2003.

Option Vertical Call Debit Spread
    Buy October 20 Call   (2.55)
    Sell October 25 Call   <u>0.85</u>
                Net Debit   (1.70)

Switch Vertical (Bull) Credit Spread
    Buy December Single Stock Future   (20.90)
    ELX Close   <u>20.86</u>
        Single Stock Future "Premium"   (0.04)
        Sell October Call   <u>0.85</u>
                Net Credit   0.81

Breakeven Points
- Option Spread
        Lower Strike   20.00
        plus Net Debit   <u>1.70</u>
               Option Spread BEP   21.70
- Switch Spread
        Cost of December Single Stock Future   20.90
        minus Net Credit   <u>(0.85)</u>
               Switch Spread BEP   20.05

Maximum Limited Potential Gain
- Option Spread

Difference Between the Strikes	5.00	
minus Net Debit	(1.70)	
Option Spread Maximum Potential Gain		3.30

- Switch Spread

Strike of Purchased Call	25.00	
minus Cost Basis of Single Stock Future	(20.05)	
Switch Spread Maximum Potential Gain		4.95

Initial In-The-Money Status
- Option Spread In-The-Money Status

ELX Close	20.86	
minus Option Spread BEP	(21.70)	
Option Spread In-The-Money Status		(0.84)

- Switch Spread In-The-Money Status

ELX Close	20.86	
minus Switch Spread BEP	(20.05)	
Switch Spread In-The-Money Status		0.81

The net debit and, therefore, the maximum possible loss of the option spread, are equal to the net debit of 1.70. The maximum possible gain is equal to the difference between the strikes minus the net debit (3.30). The October expiration date was used to provide enough time for the position to become profitable. Of course what usually happens is, I select October and the underlying doesn't move until November or, as in this case, I select October and the position reaches its maximum profit before September expiration.

Using a switch spread instead of the vertical call debit spread means that the 2.55 debit for the premium paid on the October 20 long call is replaced by a 0.04 debit which is the difference between the 20.90 fair value of the single stock future and the 20.86 price of the underlying ELX stock. This makes the switch spread start 0.81 in-the-money while the option spread starts out-of-the-money by 0.84. When ELX is at 20.00, the option debit spread is at its maximum loss point of 1.70 while the switch credit spread is only 0.05 below its breakeven point.

The profit and loss comparison is, perhaps, best graphically illustrated by **FIGURE 9.2**. The heavy solid black line presents the gain/loss graph for the switch credit spread. The thin black line presents the gain/loss graph for the options debit spread. The maximum potential loss for the option debit spread is 1.70. However, the maximum potential loss for the switch credit spread is unlimited down to zero for the underlying ELX. This represents a potential loss of 20.06 for the switch spread versus 1.70 for the option spread.

FIGURE 9.2: GAIN/LOSS COMPARISON OPTION VERTICAL CALL DEBIT SPREAD
AND EQUIVALENT SWITCH CREDIT SPREAD

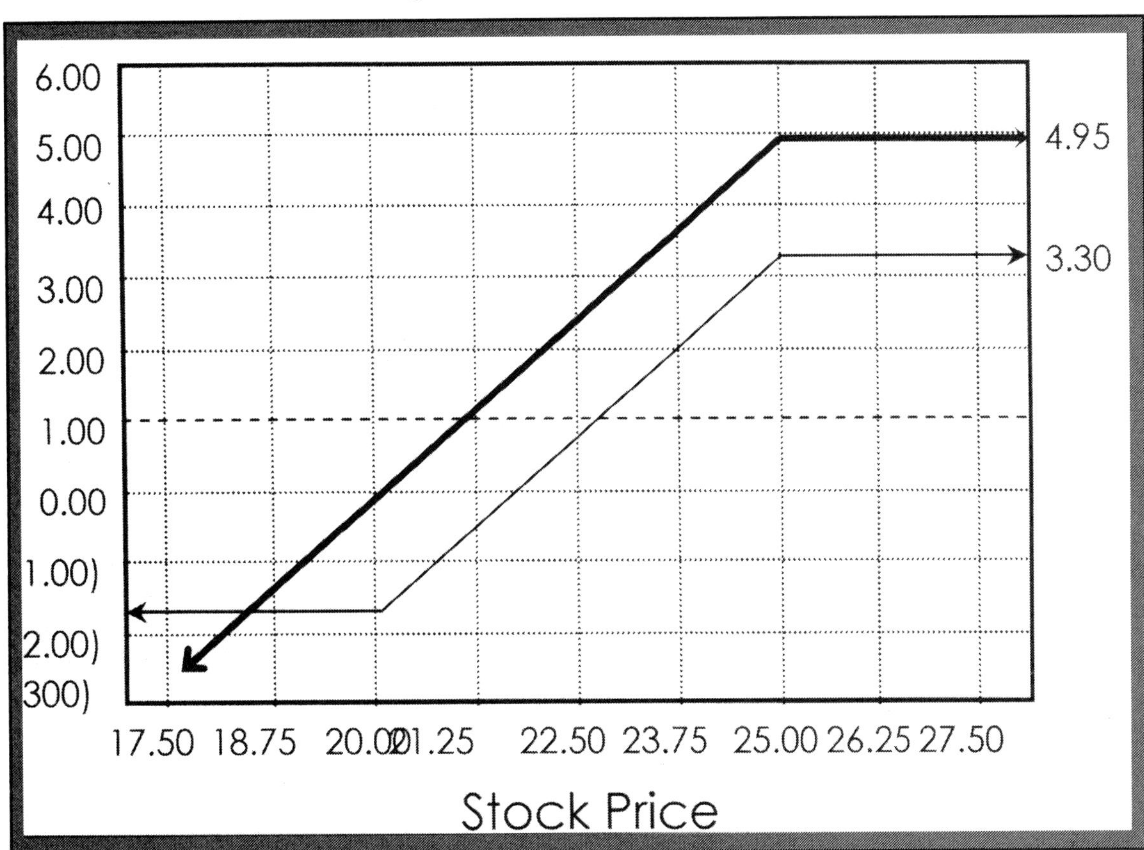

The unlimited potential loss of the switch spread must be handled by using an initial protective stop and other position management techniques.

POSITION MANAGEMENT CONSIDERATIONS

In general, the initial breakeven point of the switch spread provides a good first estimate of an initial protective stop. If this proves too close to the opening price of the single stock future, then the price of the single stock future minus the net debit of the option vertical call debit spread provides a good initial protective stop. In this case, 20.09 is probably too close for an initial protective stop. The point where the switch spread loss equals the maximum loss of the vertical call debit spread, or 18.39, would provide more room to avoid being whipsawed out of the position. This would make the reward/risk ratio for the option spread 1.9 (3.30/1.70) and the risk reward ratio for the switch spread 2.9 (4.94/1.70). This initial protective stop is consistent with the setup information in Figure 5.1. The vertical call debit spread does not require a protective stop; however, many traders prefer to take defensive action when the position moves against them. I prefer to close the position while the long call still has some time value.

The bull vertical debit spread and the equivalent switch spread have a short position that should be carefully monitored. Although the short position in the option spread is covered, the transaction costs involved in being exercised can seriously cut into any profits. Therefore, as the underlying approaches the upper strike, I prefer a protective stop based on the price of the underlying. If your broker doesn't provide this alternative for placing stops on options, I suggest you seriously consider finding a broker that does.

For a highly volatile stock, another defensive action if the position moves against you is to leave the short call open, leave the long single stock future open, and purchase a long out-of-the-money put as insurance for the long single stock future. Experienced traders may want to use this strategy rather than risk being whipsawed out of a potentially profitable position. This strategy increases the net debit and should only be used by experienced traders.

CONCLUSION

The vertical call debit spread is the most commonly used spread. It consists of a long option at or near the money and a short option with a higher strike. Both options must be on the same underlying stock and have the same expiration dates. The credit received from the sale of the short option is used to partially offset the cost of the higher priced long option. The initial position results in a net debit to your account. This chapter discusses a strategy called a switch bull credit spread. When coupled with an initial protective stop and good position management techniques, a switch bull credit spread provides increased profit potential with a better risk/reward ratio.

A word of caution: *If good position management practices
are not used, catastrophic losses can occur.*

REFERENCES

Allure, Marc [2003]. *The Option Strategist.* New York: McGraw-Hill.

Angell, George. [1983]. *Sure Thing Options Trading.* New York: Plume (Penguin Group.)

Crask, Mitch [2003]. "Single Stock Futures Add a New Twist to Options Play." *Stocks, Futures, Options,* 2, 11 (November), pp. 42-46.

McMillan, Lawrence G. [2002]. *Options as a Strategic Investment. 4th Edition.* New York: New York Institute of Finance.

McMillan, Lawrence G. [2002]. *Profit with Options.* New York: John Wiley & Sons.

Nison, Steve [2001]. *Japanese Candlestick Charting Techniques 2nd Edition.* New York: New York Institute of Finance

Nison, Steve [1994]. *Beyond Candlesticks.* New York: John Wiley & Sons.

Williams, Michael S., and Amy Hoffman [2001]. *Fundamentals of the Options Market.* New York: McGraw-Hill.

Appendix A has a summary of order types. Appendix B has a summary of most option strategies. Appendix C has the various expiration cycles.

Zelkin, Marvin H. [2002]. *It's Your Option: A Trader's Primer.* Greenville, SC: Traders Press, Inc.

CHAPTER TEN

STRANGLES

OVERVIEW OF STRANGLES

A short strangle involves the sale of puts and is excluded by the screening criteria in Chapter Three. Therefore, only long strangles are discussed. The difference between a straddle (Chapter Eight) and a strangle is one of degree not kind. A straddle is the purchase of a put and a call, usually-at-the-money, with the same strikes and the same expiration dates. With XYZ stock selling at 89.50, a typical straddle would be the simultaneous purchase of an XYZ May 90 put and an XYZ May 90 call. A long strangle is the purchase of a put and a call, usually out-of-the-money, with different strikes and the same expiration dates. With XYZ stock selling at 89.50, a typical strangle would be the simultaneous purchase of an XYZ May 85 put and an XYZ May 95 call.

Straddle
> Stock XYZ at 89.50
> Buy May 90 put
> Buy May 90 call

Strangle - Long
> Stock XYZ price 89.50
> Buy May 85 put
> Buy May 95 call

Like the long straddle, the long strangle is used when an increase in volatility is expected and the trader is uncertain about the direction of the price move. The upside is the strangle has a lower net debit and, therefore, less risk. The downside is the underlying must make a more dramatic price move to become profitable. If correct, the reward is unlimited. Maximum loss is limited to the cost of the put and the call.

When a technical setup points to a probable move with the direction uncertain, often the implied volatilities of the out-of-the-money options are higher than the volatility of the underlying. This is because everyone can see that the stock has a low volatility and they are expecting an increase in volatility. On March 12, 2003, American International Group (AIG) closed at 44.70. The volatilities and prices of AIG, the May 40 put and the May 50 call are given below.

Instrument	Volatility	Close
AIG	0.380	44.70
May 40 put	0.532	1.80
May 50 call	0.403	1.30

The implied volatilities of the options indicate the market thinks AIG is going to experience a volatility increase in the near-term. Long strangles with high volatility options are seldom profitable for three reasons. First, the anticipated increase in volatility may not occur. Second, the increase in volatility may occur after the options expire. Third, the underlying has to move too far to cover the premium on both the call and the put. In this case, the net debit to open the strangle is 3.10. The zone of loss from 36.90 to 53.10 covers a rather large area. This means a trader could open the strangle, be correct in the analysis, and lose money.

THE OPTION STRANGLE

The setup forming the basis of this chapter is identical to the AIG daily chart in Figure 8.1. This chart is reproduced as **FIGURE 10.1**. The relevant material related to Figure 10.1 is repeated from Chapter Eight. The thick solid line at the top (see arrow) represents strong, long term crossover support to resistance which was formed before the beginning of the daily chart. This line was drawn

FIGURE 10.1: AIG STRANGLE SETUP

based on a long-term weekly chart. The top of the first down gap is represented by the dashed line. Solid lines indicate the tops and bottoms of long black bodies. Dotted lines represent the midpoints of long black bodies. The rectangle in the lower right-hand corner identifies a candlestick pattern called an unconfirmed morning star. The bottom two solid lines and the bottom dotted line are not drawn based on a long black body. This is because three consecutive down long black bodies are considered as one, long, three-day black body. Combining candles in this manner prevents cluttering the chart with lines and also increases the robustness of the analysis.

The Doji morning star on March 12, 2003 represents an excellent place for a strangle because it could be signaling the beginning of an uptrend. If this occurs AIG could experience a significant upward move and the long call could become profitable. However the morning star has not been confirmed on March 12th. As a result, there is a chance that the downtrend could continue. If this happens, a significant downward move could result and the long put could become profitable. The expectation is that AIG will probably make a significant move in one direction or the other. The opening data for the option strangle on March 12, 2003 are provided below.

AIG Option Strangle Opening Data

May 40 Put	(1.80)	
plus May 50 Call	(1.30)	
Net Debit		(3.10)

The breakeven points are calculated below.

May 50 Strike	50.00	
plus net debit	3.10	
High BEP		53.10
May 40 strike	40.00	
minus net debit	3.10	
Low BEP		36.90

On April 23, 2003, the technical pattern suggested a good closing point. The closing data for the option strangle that closed on April 23, 2003 is provided below.

AIG Option Strangle Closing Data

May 40 Put	0.05	
plus May 50 Call	8.80	
Net Credit		8.85
Original Debit		(3.10)
Net Gain from Option Strangle		5.75

The net gain from the option strangle is 5.75 for an actual reward/risk ratio of 1.9. There are two switch versions of this strangle: (i) buy the single stock future and buy the May 40 put and (ii) short the single stock future and buy the May 50 call.

SWITCH STRANGLE WITH LONG SINGLE STOCK FUTURE

One version of the switch strangle involves switching a long single stock future which is close to the 45.00 strike for the May 50.00 call and buying the May 40.00 put. This position is used when the trader has a bullish bias. In this case, the setup lines indicate a bullish bias so this is the alternative of choice. The March 12, 2003 opening prices for this switch strangle are given below.

Open AIG Switch Strangle With A Long Single Stock Future On March 12, 2003.

May 40 Put		(1.80)
May Single Stock Future Close	44.75	
AIG Close	44.70	
Single Stock Future Premium	(0.05)	
Net Debit		(1.85)

The net debit for the switch strangle is reduced from 3.10 to 1.85. This has a direct effect on the breakeven points.

Switch Strangle BEP Up

AIG Close	44.70
plus Net Debit	1.85
BEP Up	46.55

Position management and downside potential is managed like the long switch straddle in Chapter Eight. The net debit is reduced from 3.10 to 1.85. The risk of the option strangle is limited to the net debit of 3.10. However, the switch strangle with a long single stock future has a maximum downside risk which is equal to the protection provided by the long May 40 put minus the cost of the long May 40 put.

Maximum Loss of Switch Strangle With Long Single Stock Future

May Single Stock Future	(44.75)
Strike of May 40 Put	40.00
Loss from Long Single Stock Future	(4.75)
Cost Of Long May 40 Put	(1.80)
Maximum Loss	(6.55)

This switch strangle should be placed by first opening the long May 40 put and then opening long the single stock future. This provides protection against the unlimited downside loss on the single stock future that would occur if the single stock future were opened first. The long future should be opened with a limit order to guarantee a maximum price. If the future cannot be opened quickly, the switch strangle should not be placed. The initial protective stop for the long single stock future should be triggered if the morning star pattern fails to be confirmed. The reason is the long single stock future must be closed before the long put can generate any gains. The long white, up gap bar the day after the entry bar (see arrow Figure 10.2) is a rising window that provides confirmation of the Doji morning star. Therefore, the initial protective stop should be cancelled and trailing protective stops on the upside should be used to help protect part of the profits. The results of holding the switch strangle as long as the option strangle (until April 23, 2003), are provided below.

Close AIG Switch Strangle With a Long Single Stock Future on April 23, 2003

May 40 Put	0.05	
Close May Single Stock Future	58.31	
Total Cash In		58.36
minus BEP Up		(46.55)
Net Gain		11.81

The gain from the switch strangle (11.81) is twice the gain from the option strangle (5.75). The additional gain comes with an additional downside risk that, percentage wise, is equal to the upside gain. The switch strangle has a downside risk that is almost twice as large as the option strangle. The put is closed to provide a benchmark. In practice the long May 40 put would have been left open.

SWITCH STRANGLE WITH SHORT SINGLE STOCK FUTURE

A second version of the switch strangle involves switching a short single stock future which is close to the 45.00 strike for the May 40 call and buying the May 50 call. This position is used when the trader has a bearish bias. In this case, this alternative would also be used for a truly neutral bias because the short single stock future would be switched for the option with the highest implied volatility. The March 12, 2003 opening prices for the switch strangle with a short single stock future are given below.

Open AIG Switch Strangle With a Short Single Stock Future on March 12, 2003

May Single Stock Future	44.75
minus AIG Close	(44.70)
Single Stock Future Premium	0.05
May 50 Call	(1.30)
Net Debit	(1.25)

Maximum Loss of Switch Strangle With Short Single Stock Future

Strike of May 50 Call	(50.00)	
Price of Short Single Stock Future	44.75	
Loss from Short Single Stock Future		(5.25)
Cost of Long May 50 Call		(1.25)
Maximum Loss		(6.50)

Position management and upside potential must be managed like the short switch straddle in Chapter Eight. The net debit is reduced from 3.10 to 1.25. The risk of the option strangle is limited to the net debit of 3.10. The maximum risk of the switch strangle with the short single stock future is the protection provided by the long May 50 call plus the cost of the long May 50 call. The switch strangle with a short single stock future is managed differently than the switch strangle with a long single stock future.

This switch strangle should be placed by first opening the long May 50 call and then shorting the single stock future. This prevents an uncovered short single stock future and is possible because the single stock future can be shorted on a down tick. The initial protective stop for the short single stock future should be triggered if the morning star pattern is confirmed. The long white, up gap bar the day after the entry bar (see arrow) is a rising window that provides confirmation of the Doji morning star (**FIGURE 10.2**).

FIGURE 10.2: SWITCH STRANGLE CLOSE SHORT SINGLE STOCK FUTURE

It cost 47.80 to repurchase the short single stock future. The results of the switch strangle with a short single stock future are provided below.

Open Short Single Stock Future	44.75	
Close Short Single Stock Future	(47.80)	
Net Loss on Single Stock Future		(3.05)
Open May 50 Call	(1.30)	
Close May 50 Call	8.80	
Net Gain on Call		7.50
Net Gain on Short Switch Strangle		4.45

The short single stock future switch alternative did not perform as well as the long single stock future alternative because AIG reversed to an uptrend rather than continuing the downtrend.

CONCLUSION

The difference between a straddle (Chapter Eight) and a strangle is one of degree not kind. A straddle is the purchase of a put and a call, usually-at-the-money, with the same strikes and the same expiration dates. A long strangle is the simultaneous purchase of an out-of-the-money put and an out-of-the money call with the same expiration dates. It is important to purchase a strangle for a specified net debit. The switch version of a strangle works best when the trader has a neutral to a slight directional bias. When the directional bias is slightly bullish go long the single stock future. When the directional bias is slightly bearish, go short the single stock future. When there is no directional bias, construct a switch strangle with the smallest net debit that is consistent with the implied volatilities of the breakeven points (See Chapter Seven, Long Condor Spreads).

REFERENCES

Allure, Marc [2003]. *The Option Strategist.* New York: McGraw-Hill.

Angell, George. [1983]. *Sure Thing Options Trading.* New York: Plume Penguin Group.

McMillan, Lawrence G. [2002]. *Options as a Strategic Investment. 4th Edition.* New York: New York Institute of Finance.

McMillan, Lawrence G. [2002]. *Profit with Options.* New York: John Wiley & Sons.

Nison, Steve [2001]. *Japanese Candlestick Charting Techniques 2nd Edition.* New York: New York Institute of Finance

Nison, Steve [1994]. *Beyond Candlesticks.* New York: John Wiley & Sons.

Williams, Michael S., and Amy Hoffman [2001]. *Fundamentals of the Options Market.* New York: McGraw-Hill.

Appendix A has a summary of order types. Appendix B has a summary of most option strategies. Appendix C has the various expiration cycles.

Zelkin, Marvin H. [2002]. *It's Your Option: A Trader's Primer.* Greenville, SC: Traders Press, Inc.

CHAPTER ELEVEN

BUTTERFLY SPREADS

OVERVIEW OF BUTTERFLY SPREADS

The goal of the butterfly spread is to create a position at little or no cost with an excellent reward/risk ratio. The butterfly spread has limited risk and limited potential gain. A long butterfly spread involves buying one contract at the lowest and highest of three consecutive strikes and selling two contracts at the middle strike. Because the screening criteria in Chapter Three specifically exclude short puts, only butterfly call spreads are discussed. Butterfly spreads can have a directional bias or a neutral outlook. With XYZ stock selling at 80, an example of a slightly bullish bias butterfly spread would be long one XYZ 80 call, short two XYZ 85 calls and long one XYZ 90 call. A more aggressively bullish spread would start at the 85 strike. With XYZ stock selling at 80, an example of a neutral butterfly call spread would be long an XYZ 75 call, short two XYZ 80 calls and long one XYZ 85 call. In each case all calls would have the same expiration date. The butterfly spread is a combination of a vertical call debit spread and a vertical call credit spread. Therefore, gain is limited to the difference between two consecutive strikes minus the net debit. In other words, the maximum gain occurs when the underlying closes at the middle strike. The maximum risk is the net debit generated when the position is opened.

To see how this works, take a butterfly spread with a net debit of 1.15 and three calls with one long 75 call, two short 80 calls and one long 85 call. When the underlying closes at 75, all of the calls expire worthless and the loss equals the original net debit of 1.15. When the underlying closes at 85, the long 85 call expires worthless, and the 10.00 gain from the long 75 call is exactly off set by the 10.00 loss from repurchasing the two short calls at 5.00 each. Therefore, the net loss is equal to the original net debit of 1.15. When the underlying closes at the middle strike of 80, the long 75 call is worth 5.00 and all other calls expire worthless and the net gain on the spread equals the difference between the 75 and 80 strikes (5.00) minus the net debit of 1.15 or 3.85. This represents the maximum gain that can be taken from the butterfly spread. For example, when the underlying closes at 79.00, the gain from closing the long 75 call is 4.00 and all other calls expire worthless. Subtracting the original 1.15 net debit from the 4.00 gain resulting from closing the spread yields a 2.85 net gain for the butterfly spread. In like manner, when the underlying closes at 81.00, the closing gain of 6.00 from the long 75 call is decreased by the 2.00 cost of closing both short 80 calls (2 calls at 1.00 each). Once again, subtracting the original 1.15 net debit from the 4.00 gain from closing the spread yields a 2.85 net gain for the butterfly spread. Therefore, the maximum gain for the long butterfly spread occurs when the underlying closes at the middle strike.

Switch spreads work best for long call butterfly spreads with a slightly bullish bias where the underlying is selling near the lower strike. One such situation occurred on August 6, 2003 when IBM closed at 79.75. IBM had been trading between 80 and 90 for five months. The expectation was IBM would go from 80 to 85 in the next six weeks with a potential upside price of 90. A long butterfly spread using one long 80 call, two short 85calls and one long 90 call looked like a good trade. The strategy was to close the long 80 call and the short 85 calls when IBM broke 85. This would generate a gain and result in holding the remaining long 90 call for free. This call should be closed either two weeks before September expiration or when IBM gives a topping candle pattern 90, whichever comes first (Figure 11.1).

COMPARISON OF OPTION AND SWITCH BUTTERFLY SPREADS

A comparison of the option butterfly spread with the equivalent switch butterfly spread is provided below.

- Option Butterfly Spread
  Buy One Sep. 80 Call (2.75)
  Sell Two Sep. 85 Calls 1.90 (2 @0.95)
  Buy One Sep. 90 Call <u>(0.30)</u>
    Option Butterfly Spread Net Debit (1.15)
- Switch Butterfly Spread
  Buy One Single Stock Future
    Single Stock Future Price (79.85)
    IBM price <u>79.75</u>
     Single Stock Future "Premium" (0.10)
  Sell Two Sep 85 Calls 1.90 (2 @ 0.95)
  Buy One Sep 90 Call <u>(0.30)</u>
    Switch Butterfly Spread Net Credit 1.50

The breakeven point for the option spread is 81.15 (net debit plus lowest strike) while the breakeven point for the switch spread is 78.35 (single stock future price minus the net credit of 1.50). There was short-term support about 78.70, so 78.35 looked like a good point for an initial protective stop for the single stock future. The price where the switch spread loss equals the option loss is 77.20 (switch BEP, 78.35, minus option net debit of 1.15). This should provide room for execution slippage incase IBM blew by the initial protective stop at 78.35. These considerations illustrate the position management strategies of a butterfly switch spread that are needed to offset the unlimited potential loss of the switch spread when compared to the limited loss of the option butterfly spread.

BUTTERFLY SPREAD RISK MANAGEMENT

A screen capture of the complete butterfly spread trade is found in Figure 11.1. The solid black line on the top chart is the bottom of a down gap. The next three dashed lines represent the top middle and bottom of two consecutive long black bodies and the bottom dashed line represents long-term support at the top of a long white body. The solid vertical line and the price data in the upper left-hand corner of all four charts provide data for the day the spread is opened which is August 8, 2003. The first vertical dashed line is September 2, 2003 which is the day to close the two short 85 calls and the long 80 call. The second vertical dashed line is September 9, 2003 which is the day to close the remaining long 90 call.

FIGURE 11.1: IBM BUTTERFLY SPREAD SCREEN CAPTURE

When there is no volatility skew and no change in the implied volatilities over the life of the spread, generating a gain using a butterfly option spread is primarily based upon the delta of the three positions. As the stock increases in price the delta of the long lowest strike will always be greater than the higher strike, out-of-the-money short calls at the middle strike. This means that for a one dollar increase in the underlying, the lowest strike, which is always more in-the-money, will increase in value more than the two short calls. However, as the underlying approaches the middle strike the difference in the rate of change of delta (gamma) for the two short positions begins to increase faster than the lowest long strike. At some point, depending upon the implied volatility, the loss from repurchasing the two short calls will exceed the gain from selling the long lower strike call. This usually happens slightly above the strike of the middle calls. The idea is to close the long lowest call and the two short calls for a profit before this happens. Closing these positions at a gain covers the initial debit and provides a profit. This locks in a minimum gain with an additional potential gain from the long call that is still open. Any gain from the remaining open long call is all profit because the cost of the spread has already been covered. Here time decay kicks in and begins to influence all other factors. The mathematics of the curvilinear time-decay function indicates a good final exit point for the remaining long call is ten trading days or two calendar weeks before expiration. Below is a comparison of option and switch spreads managed in this manner.

Option Butterfly Spread

option	open	close	gain/(loss)
Sep 80 call	(2.75)	6.10	3.35
Sep 85 call	1.90	(4.40)	(2.50)
Sep 90 call	(0.30)	1.15	0.85
	Option Butterfly Spread Gain		1.70

Switch Butterfly Spread

option	open	close	gain/(loss)
Single Stock Future	(79.85)	85.89	6.04
Sep 85 call	1.90	(4.40)	(2.50)
Sep 90 call	(0.30)	1.15	0.85
	Switch Butterfly Spread Gain		4.39

The gain from the option butterfly spread is a respectable 1.70. However, the gain from the switch butterfly spread is 4.39 for an increased return of one hundred fifty-eight percent.

WHY THE SWITCH BUTTERFLY SPREAD WORKS

The single stock future has a delta at, or close to, 1.0, therefore, except for the spread between the bid and the ask, the single stock future captures the entire upward move of IBM. The September 80 option has a delta less than 1.0 and therefore realizes a percentage of the entire move. The fair value of the single stock future is not influenced by volatility. As expiration approaches, the time premium of all options falls toward zero. Since the fair value of a single stock future does not have a time component, time decay does not affect its value.

Under most circumstances the option version of this butterfly spread would not be opened for two reasons:
- The goal of zero debit or credit is violated.
- The reward/risk ratio is too low.

HOW VOLATILITY AFFECTS A SWITCH BUTTERFLY SPREAD

The switch spread has a net credit of 1.50 which affords some downside protection if the position moves against you. With a net debit of 1.15, the option butterfly spread violates the basic purpose of butterfly spreads which is to start with a net debit close to zero. However, this is not the whole story. Volatility also plays a role.

The relevant information is provided below:

	volatility	fair value	price	overpayment
IBM	0.213		79.75	
Single Stock Future	n/a		79.85	0.10
Sep 80 call	0.243	2.44	2.75	0.31
Sep 85 call	0.238	0.73	0.95	0.22
Sep 90 call	0.248	0.16	0.30	0.14

The overpayment for the September 80 call and the September 90 call is exactly offset by the income from the sale of the two September calls. This is an example where the facts fit the theory. The overpayment of the 0.45 for the September 90 and the September 80 long calls is offset by the extra 0.44 received from the sale of the two September 85 calls. (Well not exactly, but who is going to quibble over one penny?) When the implied volatility of the options is more than the volatility of the underlying stock it is assumed that the extra amount paid for the long positions is offset by the income received from the short positions. This example is a good illustration of such a situation. Under these circumstances the option spread would be considered.

The switch version removes all doubt. The switch butterfly spread changes the underpayment/overpayment breakeven situation to an initial underpayment. It works this way: view the additional 0.10 cost of the single stock future as an overpayment, add to this the 0.14 overpayment for the September 90 call making a total overpayment for the long positions of 0.24. Subtract from this amount the 0.44 (0.22 x 2) received from the sale of the two September 85 calls. The sum of the all overpayments results in an "underpayment" of 0.20. Therefore, the switch spread results in an underpayment for the options of 0.24. For an illustration of how this works see [Mendoza 2004].

CONCLUSION

The most common butterfly spread uses options with three consecutive strikes and the expectation that the stock price will settle around the middle strike. This spread is usually opened with a neutral outlook when the underlying is trading at or near the middle strike. Switch spreads work best for long call butterfly spreads with a slightly bullish bias where the underlying is selling near the lower strike.

The switch butterfly spread has three advantages over the option butterfly spread:
- It has greater profit potential.
- It is opened for a net credit rather than a net debit.
- The option legs of the switch spread result in the equivalent of an underpayment for the option legs.

There are two disadvantages:
- Increased margin is required.
- There is unlimited downside risk that must be properly managed to avoid catastrophic loss.

REFERENCES

Allure, Marc [2003]. *The Option Strategist.* New York: McGraw-Hill.

Angell, George. [1983]. *Sure Thing Options Trading.* New York: Plume (Penguin Group.

Crask, Mitch [2003]. Single Stock Futures Add a New Twist to Options Play. *Stocks, Futures, Options,* 2, 11 (November), pp. 42-46.

McMillan, Lawrence G. [2002]. *Options as a Strategic Investment. 4th Edition.* New York: New York Institute of Finance.

McMillan, Lawrence G. [2002]. *Profit with Options.* New York: John Wiley & Sons.

Nison, Steve [2001]. *Japanese Candlestick Charting Techniques 2nd Edition.* New York: New York Institute of Finance

Nison, Steve [1994]. *Beyond Candlesticks.* New York: John Wiley & Sons.

Williams, Michael S., and Amy Hoffman [2001]. *Fundamentals of the Options Market.* New York: McGraw-Hill.

Appendix A has a summary of order types. Appendix B has a summary of most option strategies. Appendix C has the various expiration cycles.

Zelkin, Marvin H. [2002]. *It's Your Option: A Trader's Primer.* Greenville, SC: Traders Press, Inc.

CHAPTER TWELVE

THE IRON BUTTERFLY

OVERVIEW OF THE IRON BUTTERFLY

The short iron butterfly results in a net credit and does not provide many opportunities for a viable switch alternative. The long iron butterfly is considered a complex strategy because it is constructed by buying an at-the-money call and an at-the-money put (or a long straddle) and selling an out-of-the-money put and an out-of-the-money call (or a short strangle). This strategy is best explained using an example.

On July 3, 2003 Wal-Mart Stores, Inc. (WMT) closed at 54.96. The long iron butterfly details are listed below:

Long At-The-Money Straddle
       Buy September 55 put   (2.35)
       Buy September 55 call <u>(2.35)</u>
             Debit   (4.70)
Short Out-Of-The-Money Strangle
       Sell September 50 put   0.85
       Sell September 60 call <u>0.45</u>
             Credit   <u>1.30</u>
        Option Iron Butterfly Net Debit   (3.40)

FIGURE 12.1: SCREEN CAPTURE OF IRON BUTTERFLY OPEN

The switch iron butterfly uses a short put. This does not violate the screening criteria in Chapter Three because the long September 55 put provides insurance for the short September 50 put. For example, if the underlying is put to the trader at 50, the trader can, in turn, put the stock to another trader at 55. Admittedly this results in a loss. However, the risk is not unlimited and the trader does not end up with an unwanted stock that is going down.

For the option iron butterfly, the maximum loss is limited to the net debit of 3.40 and occurs when WMT is trading at the middle strikes of 55. The maximum gain is limited to the difference between the straddle strike and either of the strangle strikes minus the net debit. In the Wal-Mart example, the maximum gain is limited to 1.60. The maximum gain occurs when WMT is trading at either the highest strike (60) or the lowest strike (50). The upper breakeven point is the middle strike plus the net debit (58.40) and the lower breakeven point is equal to the middle strike minus the net debit (51.60).

The option iron butterfly makes money whenever the stock moves in either direction. Like the straddle (Chapter Eight), an iron butterfly is used when an increase in volatility is expected with the direction of the move unknown. The advantage of the iron butterfly is the decreased risk. In the Wal-Mart example, the long at-the-money straddle has a net debit of 4.70 which is decreased to 3.40 by selling the short out-of-the-money strangle for 1.30. However, the decreased risk comes at a price.

The straddle has an unlimited maximum gain while the iron butterfly has a limited maximum gain. Therefore, when the trader expects a large increase in volatility, the straddle would be the spread of choice.

The option iron butterfly has no directional bias. However the switch iron butterfly has a directional bias. There is a bullish bias when a long single stock future is switched for the long straddle call and a bearish bias when a short single stock future is switched for the long straddle put. Therefore, when there is truly no directional bias, the switch iron butterfly should be avoided.

LONG SINGLE STOCK FUTURE SWITCH IRON BUTTERFLY SPREAD

The long single stock future switch version of the iron butterfly is provided below.

Long Switch Straddle
    Switch September Single Stock Future for September 55 Call.
        Underlying Stock   54.96
        September Single Stock Future   (54.98)
                Single Stock Future Premium   (0.02)
            September 55 Put   (2.35)
                Net Debit for Switch Straddle   (2.37)
Short Strangle
        September 60 Call   0.45
        September 50 Put   0.85
                Credit For Strangle   1.30
                    Switch Iron Butterfly Net Debit   (1.07)

The switch iron butterfly will always have an initial net debit less than the option iron butterfly. When the underlying closes at the middle strike the loss equals the net debit for both the option and the switch versions of the iron butterfly as shown below.

Expiration Price = 55.00
    Value of Short 50 Put   0.00
    Gain from Long Single Stock Future   0.02
    Value of Long 55 Put   0.00
    Value of Short 60 Call   0.00
                                                    0.02
        Net Debit   (1.07)
                    Net loss   (1.05)

The net loss of 1.05 is 0.02 less than the net debit because the single stock future is purchased for 54.98 rather than the strike price of 55.00. Therefore, for the switch iron butterfly spread, the loss at the middle strike equals the net debit adjusted for the difference between the cost of the single stock future and the middle strike.

UPSIDE POSITION MANAGEMENT

The upside maximum gain price for both the option and the switch iron butterfly with a long single stock future occurs at the highest strike of 60. However, while the point of maximum gain is the same, the dollar value is always higher for the switch iron butterfly spread as is illustrated below.

Expiration Price = 60.00

Value of Short 50 Put	0.00
Gain from Long Single Stock Future	5.02
Value of Long 55 Put	0.00
Value of Short 60 Call	0.00

	5.02
Original Net Debit	(1.07)
Switch Iron Butterfly Maximum Gain	3.95
Option Iron Butterfly Maximum Gain	1.60

When WMT goes up the maximum gain occurs at the highest strike for both the option and the switch iron butterfly. The upside breakeven point for the option iron butterfly equals the net debit plus the middle strike. The upside breakeven point for the switch iron butterfly spread is equal to the cost of the long single stock future plus the net debit. Here is where the similarity of the calculations between the option iron butterfly spread and the switch iron butterfly spread with a long single stock future end. There is a significant difference on the downside.

DOWNSIDE POSITION MANAGEMENT

When WMT goes down the maximum gain for the option iron butterfly occurs when WMT reaches the lower 50 strike. However, for the switch iron butterfly with a long single stock future, when WMT reaches 50.00 the switch spread loss is the same as the loss at the middle strike. The relevant calculations are provided below.

Expiration Price = 50.00

Value of Short 50 Put	0.00
Loss from Long Single Stock Future	(4.98)
Value of Long 55 Put	5.00
Value of Short 60 Call	0.00

	0.02
Net Debit	(1.07)
Net Loss	(1.05)

The reason the switch iron butterfly with a long single stock future does not make any money on the downside is the gain on the long put is exactly offset by the loss on the long single stock future.

Why bother with a switch iron butterfly spread? As long as the price move is large enough, the option spread makes money no matter which direction the underlying moves. On the other hand, the switch spread requires a directional bias. The key part of the statement is "as long as the price move is large enough." When there is no directional bias, the iron butterfly switch spread should be avoided. However, when a trader has some directional bias the switch spread is the trade of choice. In the Wal-Mart illustration the maximum gain is increased from 1.60 for the option spread to 3.95 for the switch spread and the breakeven point on the upside is lowered from 58.40 to 56.05. The increased profit is illustrated by the calculations for the iron butterfly trade based on the closing prices on September 4, 2003.

COMPARISON OF OPTION IRON BUTTERFLY SPREAD AND SWITCH IRON BUTTERFLY SPREAD WITH A LONG SINGLE STOCK FUTURE

Gain from Iron Butterfly Option Spread
Straddle Portion
 Gain/(Loss) from September 55 Put (0.05)
 Gain/(Loss) from September 55 Call <u>5.20</u>
   Straddle Net Gain 5.15
Strangle Portion
 Gain/(Loss) from September 50 Put (0.05)
 Gain/(Loss) from September 60 Call <u>(0.85)</u>
   Strangle Net Loss <u>(0.90)</u>
Iron Butterfly Option Spread Gain 4.25
  Less Net Debit <u>(3.40)</u>
    NET GAIN 0.85

Gain from Iron Butterfly Switch Spread
Straddle Portion
 Gain/(Loss) from September 55 Put (0.05)
 September Single Stock Future Gain <u>5.04</u>
   Straddle Net Gain 4.99
Strangle Portion
 Gain/(Loss) from September 50 Put (0.05)
 Gain/(Loss) from September 60 Call <u>(0.85)</u>
   Strangle Net Loss <u>(0.90)</u>
Iron Butterfly Option Spread Gain 4.09
  Less Net Debit <u>(1.05)</u>
    NET GAIN 3.04

The original risk for the switch spread is thirty-one percent of the risk for the option spread (1.07÷3.40). The trading net gain for the option spread is 3.6 times greater than the gain from the option spread (3.04÷0.85). The net closing debit for the switch spread is 1.05 and not the calculated opening net debit of 1.07 because the single stock future is purchased for 54.98 rather than the strike price of 55.00.

CONCLUSION

The short iron butterfly results in a net credit and does not provide many opportunities for a viable switch alternative. The long iron butterfly is constructed by buying an at-the-money call and an at-the-money put (or a long straddle) and selling an out-of-the-money put and an out-of-the-money call (or a short strangle).

For the option iron butterfly, the maximum loss is limited to the net debit and occurs when the underlying is trading at the middle strikes of the long straddle. The maximum gain is limited to the difference between the straddle strike and either of the strangle strikes minus the net debit. The maximum gain occurs when the underlying is trading at either the highest or the lowest strike. The upper breakeven point is the middle strike plus the net debit and the lower breakeven point is equal to the middle strike minus the net debit. The option iron butterfly makes money whenever the stock moves in either direction. However the switch iron butterfly has a directional bias. There is a bullish bias when a single stock future is switched for the long straddle call and a bearish bias when a single stock future is switched for the long straddle put.

For the switch iron butterfly with a long single stock future, the breakeven point and maximum gain calculations are different from the option iron butterfly. When the underlying goes up, the maximum gain occurs at the highest strike for both the option and the switch iron butterfly with a long single stock future. The upside breakeven point for the option iron butterfly equals the net debit plus the middle strike. The upside breakeven point for the switch iron butterfly spread is equal to the cost of the long single stock future plus the net debit. However, when the underlying goes down, the situation changes for the switch iron butterfly spread. For the option iron butterfly, the maximum loss is equal to the net debit and the option iron butterfly has a maximum profit to the downside which occurs when underlying reaches the lowest strike. However, for the switch iron butterfly, when the underlying reaches the lower strike, the loss is the same as the loss at the middle strike. This means, for the switch iron butterfly with a long single stock future, defensive action must be taken to realize a gain when the underlying decreases in value. The opposite situation exists when the switch spread contains a short single stock future.

The switch iron butterfly with a long single stock future is used when the trader has a slightly bullish bias and the switch iron butterfly with a short single stock future is used when the trader has a slight bearish bias.

The switch iron butterfly should be avoided when the trader is completely neutral about the direction of the underlying. One word of caution: *Be sure commissions do not eat up all of the profits.*

REFERENCES

Fontanills, George A [1998]. *The Options Course.* New York: John Wiley & Sons.

Excellent introduction to options. Clearly written in small, easy-to-learn steps.

Fontanills, George A. [1998]. *The Options Course Workbook: Step-By-Step Exercises and Tests to Help You Master the Options Course.* New York: John Wiley & Sons.

The title says it all. An excellent workbook that teaches how to apply the concepts in the companion text.

Williams, Michael S., and Amy Hoffman [2001]. *Fundamentals of the Options Market.* New York: McGraw-Hill.

Appendix A has summary of order types. Appendix B has a summary of most option strategies. Appendix C has the various expiration cycles.

Zelkin, Marvin H. [2002]. *It's Your Option: A Trader's Primer.* Greenville, SC: Traders Press, Inc.

CHAPTER THIRTEEN

BOX SPREADS

OVERVIEW OF BOX SPREADS

A long box spread is a combination of two vertical debit spreads: a bullish long vertical call spread and a bearish long vertical put spread. Four options are used for this spread: two calls with different strikes and the same expiration dates coupled with two puts with the same strikes and expiration dates as the calls. An example of a long box spread would be buy an XYZ 70 call and sell an XYZ 75 call while at the same time buying an XYZ 75 put and selling an XYZ 70 put. The key is to open the entire trade for a net debit that is less than the difference between the two strikes. The short box spread involves two credit spreads and, therefore, offers little opportunity for an advantageous switch version. Accordingly, a net debit box spread is used.

The purpose of the box spread is arbitrage. Arbitrage is the process of locking-in a guaranteed small profit by taking advantage of a temporary imbalance in prices. This is accomplished by purchasing and selling the same security, or equivalent securities, at different prices so that a guaranteed profit is locked-in. Finding a profitable setup for an option box spread is easier than placing the trade. One reason is transaction costs often exceed the small guaranteed net gain. A second and more common occurrence is the arbitrage situation disappears before you can take advantage of it. Other traders see the arbitrage possibilities and execute the trade before you can place your order. One way to take advantage of a situation like this is to substitute a single stock future for one of the option positions. There are two possibilities for a switch version of the option box spread. One is using a long single stock future to replace the long, lower strike call and the other is using a short single stock future to replace the long, higher strike put. On August 6, 2004, IBM provided an excellent example of an ideal setup for the long single stock future version of the box spread.

THE OPTION BOX SPREAD

An example using the closing prices of IBM on August 6, 2003 helps explain how this works. On August 6, 2003 the following prices existed:

IBM — 79.75
IBM September 80 Call – 2.75
IBM September 85 Call – 0.95
IBM September 80 Put – 2.95
IBM September 85 Put – 5.90

A box spread could be established by doing the following:

Buy IBM September 80 Call   (2.75)
Sell IBM September 85 Call   0.95
                    Net Debit   (1.80)
Buy IBM September 85 Put   (5.90)
Sell IBM September 80 Put   2.95
                    Net Debit   (2.95)
            Total Net Debit   (4.75)

The price of IBM is irrelevant because at expiration the position is worth 5.00 for a locked-in, risk-free profit of 0.25. To see how this works let's evaluate the position at expiration. If IBM is selling at 85.00 at expiration, the September 80 call is worth 5.00 and all the other options expire worthless. If IBM is selling at 80.00 at expiration, the September 85 put is worth 5.00 and all the other options expire worthless. If the stock closes between the two strikes, then both the September 80 call and the September 85 put will have an intrinsic value totaling 5.00 and the September 85 call and the September 80 put will expire worthless. The net debit is 4.75. Therefore, the guaranteed gain is 0.25. For details about the box spread see Zelkin[2002] and McMillan[2004]. Care should be taken to prevent commissions from eating the lion's share of the trading profit. One way of accomplishing this is to trade at least 10 contracts (one-thousand shares).

SWITCH BOX SPREAD WITH A LONG SINGLE STOCK FUTURE

The switch box spread with a long single stock future has a neutral to slightly bullish outlook. It is constructed by replacing the long September 80 call with a long single stock future. In this case a December single stock future is used rather than a September single stock future for three reasons. First, the cost is not significantly different because the fair value is not related to the time to expiration. Second, if desired, the long single stock future can be left open to form the basis for another switch spread. Third, any increased value of the long single stock future can be used to margin other transactions.

On August 6, 2003 the following prices existed:

IBM — 79.75

IBM Single Stock Future	79.85
IBM September 80 Call	2.75
IBM September 85 Call	0.95
IBM September 80 Put	2.95
IBM September 85 Put	5.90

A switch box spread could be established by doing the following:

Buy IBM December Single Stock Future	(79.85)
IBM Price	79.75
Option Portion of Switch Box Spread	
Sell IBM September 85 Call	0.95
Buy IBM September 85 Put	(5.90)
Sell IBM September 80 Put	2.95
Net Debit from Option Portion of Spread	(2.00)

The upside maximum gain calculation has two components:

- The difference between the two strikes minus the net debit on the option portion of the spread plus
- the difference between the lowest strike and the cost of the long single stock future.

In this case, the maximum gain is:

Difference between the Two Strikes	5.00	
minus The Net Debit on the Options	2.00	
Gain from Option Part of Spread		3.00
Lowest Option Strike	80.00	
minus The Cost of the Long		
Single Stock Future	79.85	
Gain from Single Stock Future		0.15
Maximum Gain		3.15

At first glance, the second part of the upside maximum gain calculation for the switch box spread does not seem to make sense. However, think of it this way, the focal points of the box spread are the two strikes. When the long single stock future is exactly equal to the lower strike, on the upside, it is a perfect surrogate for a long call. All the second part of the upside maximum gain calculation for the switch box spread is doing is correcting for the difference between the purchase price of the long single stock future and the lower strike. In this case, as long as the underlying stays above the lower strike, the switch box spread and the option box spread maximum calculations are the same.

To illustrate assume the prices of the IBM single stock future is 80.00 and all other prices remain the same and do the calculations for IBM closing at 85.

	opening price	closing value	net gain/(loss)
IBM Single Stock Future	(80.00)	85.00	5.00
Sell IBM September 85 Call	0.95	0.00	0.95
Buy IBM September 85 Put	(5.90)	0.00	(5.90)
Sell IBM September 80 Put	2.95	0.00	2.95
		NET GAIN	3.00

The 3.00 net gain is equal to the net debit from the option part of the spread (2.00) subtracted from the difference between the two strikes, or 5.00. Therefore, as long as the price of IBM stays above 80.00, at expiration, the switch box spread will be worth 3.15. This represents a significant increase in profit when compared to the 0.25 gain of the option box spread. The upside maximum gain calculations are provided below.

IBM = 80.00

Single Stock Future Portion of Spread
    Open Single Stock Future   (79.85)
    Close Single Stock Future   80.00
          Net Gain   **0.15**

Short September 85 Call Portion
    Open
    Sell September 85 Call   0.95
    Expires Worthless   0.00
          Net Gain   **0.95**

Vertical Debit Put Spread Portion
    Sell September 80 Put   2.95
    Expires Worthless   0.00
          Net Gain   **2.95**
    Buy September 85 Put   (5.90)
    Value at Expiration   5.00
          Net Loss   **(0.90)**
        Total Gain   **3.15**

What happens when IBM closes above the higher 85 strike? The net gain remains 3.15. The calculations below assume IBM closes at 90.00 at expiration.

IBM = 90

Single Stock Future Portion of Spread
    Open Single Stock Future   (79.85)
    Close Single Stock Future   90.00
          Net Gain   10.15

Short September 85 Call Portion
    Open
    Sell September 85 Call   0.95
    Buy September 85 Call   (5.00)
          Net Loss   (4.05)

Vertical Debit Put Spread Portion
```
    Sell September 80 Put          2.95
    Expires Worthless              0.00
                Net Gain                  2.95
    Buy September 85 Put          (5.90)
    Expires Worthless              0.00
                Net Loss                 (5.90)
                    Maximum Gain         3.15
```

Unlike the option box spread, the switch box spread can lose money. At expiration, the breakeven point for the long single stock future switch box spread is equal to 76.85. This value is equal to the maximum gain provided by the bearish vertical put debit spread plus the writing income from the short September 85 call. The calculations are provided below.

Maximum Gain from Vertical Put Debit Spread
```
        Sell IBM September 80 Put        2.95
        Buy IBM September 85 Put        (5.90)
                    Net Debit   (2.95)
```
Maximum Gain
```
        Difference between the Strikes    5.00
        minus Net Debit                  (2.95)
    Maximum Gain from Vertical Put Spread      2.05
```
Writing Income from Short September 85 Call
```
        Sell September 85 Call           0.95
        Expires Worthless                0.00
    Writing Income from Short September 85 Call     0.95
                    Total Downside Protection      3.00
```

Breakeven Point for Long Single Stock Future Switch Box Spread.
```
    Cost of Single Stock Future                79.85
    minus Downside Protection                 (3.00)
    BEP for Long Single Stock Future Switch Box Spread      76.85
```

To verify this assume IBM closes at expiration at 76.85 and do the calculations.
Breakeven Point at Expiration = 76.85
Single Stock Future Portion of Spread
```
    Open Single Stock Future   (79.85)
    Close Single Stock Future    76.85
                Net Loss            (3.00)
```
Short September 85 Call Portion
```
    Sell September 85 Call        0.95
    Expires Worthless             0.00
                Net Gain            0.95
```

Vertical Debit Put Spread Portion

Sell September 80 Put	2.95	
Buy September 80 put	(3.15)	
Net Loss		(0.20)
Buy September 85 Put	(5.90)	
Sell September 85 Put	8.15	
Net Gain		2.25
Total Gain		0.00

This is a theoretical breakeven point. It assumes all components of the trade are held to expiration. This theoretical breakeven point must be tempered by practical trading realities. The option box spread is usually held to expiration because there is a guaranteed gain with no possible loss. However, in order to protect against the unlimited downside loss of the long single stock future, it is sometimes necessary to close the long single stock future switch box spread before expiration. When the long single stock future switch box spread is closed before expiration of either the single stock future or the options, the actual breakeven point when closed prior to expiration is usually different from the theoretical breakeven point at expiration. Three factors account for this: First, the options will usually have a time value component that will make their price greater than their intrinsic value. Second, the implied volatilities of the options usually change. Third, except at expiration, the fair value of the single stock future is usually slightly different from the underlying. The impact of these factors should not be ignored. It can materially affect the breakeven point as the Position Management section clearly demonstrates.

POSITION MANAGEMENT FOR LONG SINGLE STOCK FUTURE SWITCH BOX SPREAD

On August 6, 2003, IBM was at 79.75 and had been trading between 80 and 90 for five months. The expectation was IBM would go from 80 to 85 in the next six weeks with a potential upside price of 90. There was short-term support about 78.70.

The relevant position management considerations for the switch spread are:
- December Single stock future breakeven point at expiration of the September options = 76.85
- Total Potential Net Gain = 3.15.
- Expectation = Slightly bullish up to 85.00 with possible top of 90.00.
- Downside Possibility: IBM would pause briefly and then continue down.
- Initial Protective Stop (IPS)= 78.50
- Maximum Time Anticipated to Reach IPS: Two Weeks.

The rationale for the two week time to reach 78.70 is the support at 80.00, which if not broken, will strengthen. However, if support at 80.00 is broken, then IBM should move quickly to the next support level at 78.70. The initial protective stop for the single stock future is placed below 78.70 at 78.50 to prevent being whipsawed out of a profitable trade. The next step is to calculate the value of the bearish put spread part of the box spread if IBM is at 78.50 in two weeks.

Values for the options are based on calculations using the Black-Scholes model and are based on the assumption that the put implied volatilities remain the same. This is not always a safe assumption. The volatility of the underlying IBM stock and the implied volatility of the puts will probably increase if IBM breaks out of its trading range. If IBM does reach 78.50, the expectation would be for a further downward movement to the next support level near 75.00 because both the 80.00 and the 78.70 support levels have been broken.

The results from closing all positions are given below.

First close the short September 85 call. This prevents holding a short uncovered call.

Close Short Call Portion of Spread

Sell September 85 Call	0.95	
Buy September 85 Call	(0.38)	
Net Gain		0.57

Next close the long December single stock future.

Close December IBM Single Stock Future

Open Long December Single Stock Future	(79.85)	
Estimated Fair Value if IBM is at 78.50	78.40	
on August 20, 2003.		
Net Loss	(1.45)	
Total Net Loss to This Point		(0.88)

Notice the fair value of the IBM single stock future is less than the value of the underlying IBM. This is normal. Except at expiration, the fair value of a single stock future usually differs (either higher or lower) from the value of the underlying.

Finally, close the put part of the spread by buying back the short September 80 put and selling the long September 85 put. Once again, the option values are based on calculations using the Black-Scholes model and are based on the assumption that the put implied volatilities remain the same. This is not always a safe assumption. The volatility of the underlying IBM stock and the implied volatility of the puts will probably increase if IBM breaks out of its trading range. However, it is usually the case that the actual values do not significantly differ from the theoretical values calculated in this manner.

Close Put Portion of Spread

Buy September 85 Put	(5.90)	
Sell September 85 Put	6.80	
Net Gain		0.90
Sell September 80 Put	2.95	
Buy September 80 Put	(3.14)	
Net Loss	(0.19)	
Put Spread Gain		0.71

The result of the entire trade is calculated by algebraically adding the result of the long single stock future and the long call part of the spread (minus 0.88) to the result of the put part of the spread (plus 0.71). The result is a net loss of 0.17.

Loss from Single Stock Future and Call	(0.88)
Gain from Put Part of Spread	0.71
Total Net Loss	(0.17)

Based on these inputs, closing all positions with an initial protective stop at 78.50 results in a loss of 0.17. The original break even point when the spread is held to the expiration point of the September options is 76.85. However, an early close at 78.50 resulted in a 0.17 loss. This example illustrates the impact of an early close on the breakeven point. Not a risk free investment but certainly a very low loss for a potential gain of 3.15 at an actual reward/risk ratio of 18.5 to 1.0. This example illustrates the position management considerations needed to offset the unlimited potential loss of the switch box spread when compared to the risk-free nature of the option box spread.

The long single stock future switch box has a maximum gain that is 12.6 times greater than the option box spread. It is also profitable over a greater price range. However, there is a downside. After IBM falls below the BEP of 76.85, the potential loss is unlimited down to zero for the stock. Without proper position management, therefore, the potential loss is 76.85. The long single stock future switch box spread obviously has a neutral to bullish bias. When the outlook is neutral to slightly bearish, a short single stock future switch box spread is used. In most cases, the results of shorting a security rather than going long are relatively easy to calculate. Simply reverse the process. This is not the case for the short single stock future switch box spread.

SWITCH BOX SPREAD WITH A SHORT SINGLE STOCK FUTURE

The long single stock future switch box spread uses a long single stock future to replace the at-the-money call and downside protection is provided by monies received from the short, out-of-the-money put and the bullish vertical call spread portion of the box spread. Therefore, with IBM selling near 80, the option strikes would be 80 and 85.

Original Prices for Long Single Stock Future Switch Box Spread
IBM — 79.75

IBM Single Stock Future	79.85
IBM September 80 Call	2.75
IBM September 80 Put	2.95
IBM September 85 Call	0.95
IBM September 85 Put	5.90

The flipside, or short single stock future switch box spread, uses a short single stock future to replace the at-the-money put with upside protection provided by monies received from the short, out-of-the-money put and the vertical call debit spread portion of the switch box spread. Therefore, with IBM selling near 80, the option strikes would be 80 and 75. To make the short single stock future box spread example similar to the long single stock future switch box spread, keep the same value for the options with an 80 strike and assume the 75 strike options have the same relative value as the 85 strike options. The value for the single stock future also needs to be adjusted. In the long single stock future spread the single stock future was 0.15 below the 80 strike. A comparable price for a short single stock future spread would mean the single stock future is 0.15 above the 80 strike. When these changes are made, the following prices are used.

Equivalent Prices for Short Single Stock Future Switch Box Spread.

IBM Single Stock Future	80.15
IBM September 80 Put	2.75
IBM September 80 Call	2.95
IBM September 75 Put	0.95
IBM September 75 Call	5.90

The maximum gain remains the same at 3.15. However, for the short single stock future switch box spread, the second part of the maximum gain calculation is different. Instead of subtracting the cost of the long single stock future from the lowest strike, the highest strike is subtracted from the price received for the short single stock future. As long as IBM remains below 80, at expiration, the gain on the short single stock future switch box spread is 3.15. The calculations are provided below.

Difference between the Two Strikes	5.00	
minus The Net Debit from the Options	(2.00)	
	3.00	
Cost of Single Stock Future	80.15	
minus Highest Strike	(80.00)	
	0.15	
Maximum Gain		3.15

The upside breakeven point for the short single stock future switch box spread is equal to 83.15. This value is equal to the maximum gain provided by the bullish vertical call debit spread plus the writing income from the short September 75 put. The calculations are provided below.

Maximum Gain from Vertical Call Debit Spread		
Buy IBM September 75 Call	(5.90)	
Sell IBM September 80 Call	2.95	
Net Debit	(2.95)	
Maximum Gain		
Difference between the Strikes	5.00	
minus Net Debit	(2.95)	
Maximum Gain		2.05
Writing Income from Short September 75 Put		
Sell September 75 Put	0.95	
Expires Worthless	0.00	
Writing Income		0.95
Total Upside Protection		3.00

Breakeven Point

Cost of December Single Stock Future	80.15
plus Upside Protection	3.00
Breakeven Point	83.15

RISK

Remember the objective of the **option** box spread is to lock-in a small risk-free profit regardless of the movement of the stock. However, as with most risk-free investments, this is not exactly true. Exercise of the short positions is a potential risk when the underlying moves too far outside the spread range. The costs of being exercised can have serious implications. Therefore, with the option box spread, a trader should consider closing the relevant short position when the short position becomes too far in-the-money. For example, if IBM fell to 70.00, the short September 80 puts should probably be closed. They should most certainly be closed when they reach parity with the stock. The **switch** box spread profit is considerably increased. However, if the position moves against you, proper position management before the position is opened can prevent losses and sometimes protect some or all of the profit.

CONCLUSION

A long option box spread is a combination of two vertical debit spreads: a bullish long vertical call spread and a bearish long vertical put spread. The purpose is to lock-in a guaranteed profit. The option box spread is without risk as long as exercise of the short positions does not occur. However, this risk becomes quite real when the underlying moves too far outside the spread range. The costs of being exercised can have serious implications. Therefore, a trader should consider closing a short position that becomes too far in-the-money.

The switch box spread requires one of two outlooks: either a neutral to slightly bullish outlook with a long single stock future or a neutral to slightly bearish outlook with a short single stock future. Although the switch spread increases the potential profit amount and the price range over which the spread is profitable, the switch box spread has the disadvantage of unlimited risk for the single stock future portion of the spread. Therefore, a switch box spread should not be opened if the trader is unwilling to spend the time necessary to monitor the position. Care should also be taken to prevent commissions from eating the lion's share of the trading profit. One way of accomplishing this is to trade at least 10 contracts (one-thousand shares).

REFERENCES

Allure, Marc [2003]. *The Option Strategist.* New York: McGraw-Hill.

Angell, George. [1983]. *Sure Thing Options Trading.* New York: Penguin Group.

Brach, Marion A.[2003]. *Real Options in Practice.* New York: John Wiley & Sons.
Different viewpoints on volatility, time decay and option pricing models such as Black-Scholes. Traders familiar with mathematical game theory and binomial decision trees will find this a must read for an alternative approach to option pricing.

Crask, Mitch [2003]. Single Stock Futures Add a New Twist to Options Play. *Stocks, Futures, Options,* 2, 11 (November), pp. 42-46.

McMillan, Lawrence G. [2002]. *Options as a Strategic Investment. 4th Edition.* New York: New York Institute of Finance.

McMillan, Lawrence G. [2002]. *Profit with Options.* New York: John Wiley & Sons.

Nison, Steve [2001]. *Japanese Candlestick Charting Techniques 2nd Edition.* New York: New York Institute of Finance

Nison, Steve [1994]. *Beyond Candlesticks.* New York: John Wiley & Sons.

Williams, Michael S., and Amy Hoffman [2001]. *Fundamentals of the Options Market.* New York: McGraw-Hill.
Appendix A has a summary of order types. Appendix B has a summary of most option strategies. Appendix C has the various expiration cycles.

Zelkin, Marvin H. [2002]. *It's Your Option: A Trader's Primer.* Greenville, SC: Traders Press, Inc.

CHAPTER 14

CONCLUSION

This book presents a strategy combining two derivatives to increase the profitability of option debit spreads. The basic strategy is fourfold:

- Lower position breakeven points by turning option debit positions into equivalent switch credit positions.
- Use both historical and implied volatility as a tool to increase position profitability.
- Create positions that take advantage of the time decay of options, and
- Have a plan to manage the effects of downside risk.

The strategy is called a switch spread because one of the option positions is replaced, or switched, with a futures contract. The switch spread is an option strategy using the basic concepts, outlooks, and strategies of an option debit spread or straddle. Single stock futures are used as examples because there is a price history that permits the use of actual prices rather than theoretical situations. However, the same switch spreads could be constructed based on Eurodollars.

The basis of switch spreads is the differences between options, stocks and futures which are drawn out below. Option and stock characteristics that are different from futures contracts are in bold.

- The buyer of an option has the right to demand delivery of the underlying stock anytime before the expiration date. The same is true for a futures contract.
- **The buyer of a futures contract has the obligation to take delivery of the stock at expiration.** The option purchaser does not have this obligation.
- For a limited period of time, the sale of an option contract creates an obligation to deliver the underlying stock upon demand. The same is true for a futures contract.
- **A future is considered at "fair value" when its price is consistent with the theoretical formula:**
  Fair Value = stock price x (1 + annualized interest rate - dividend).
- **For a futures contract, the market price and the theoretical price are usually very close to one another.** All of the variables in the formula for the price of a futures contract are a question of fact and can be determined. Therefore, when a futures contract is not at or near the fair market value, either wait for arbitrage to correct the situation or check the assumptions

about either the interest rate or the dividends. This is not the case for options. Theoretical prices and market prices are often different because the option formula has one variable, volatility of the underlying, which can be estimated in a statistical probability sense only.

- Both implied volatility and the volatility of the underlying have a major impact on the price of an option. **The term implied volatility has no meaning in relation to the price of a futures contract because the volatility of the underlying has no impact on the price of a futures contract.** (See the formula for the fair market value of a futures contract.)
- Time decay can become a major consideration for some option spreads. **A futures contract does not experience time decay.** (See the formula for the fair market value of a futures contract.)
- **Once the fair value is determined, the future has a delta close to or equal to 1.0.**
- **A futures contract can be shorted on a down tick. A stock cannot.**
- **A future can be shorted without borrowing the stock. A stock cannot.**
- **A single stock future has a twenty percent margin requirement.** Compare this to stocks with a twenty-five percent margin for pattern day traders and a fifty percent margin requirement for trades that are open more than one day.
- For any given underlying security, there are option alternatives with different strike prices and different expiration dates. **There may be futures contracts with different expiration dates, however, the prices are usually close to the underlying price and for each expiration date there is only one price, the fair value.**
- **Shorting a futures contract does not create a credit to your account.**

The key to the switch strategy is three of the differences between options and single stock futures. A single stock future does not experience time decay. In most cases, once the Fair value is determined, a single stock future has a delta at, or very close to 1.00. A single stock future price is not related to the volatility of the underlying stock. The impact of volatility is best illustrated when a long single stock future is switched for a long option. Because the price of the single stock future is not based on the volatility of the underlying stock, you avoid paying the high premium on the purchased call option portion of the spread; however, you still receive the high premium for the sale of the short call.

Six screening criteria are presented. They are:

1. Limit the use of the switch strategy to debit spreads and straddles where the short positions are calls.
2. As a general statement, select an underlying with a market price that has a favorable relationship to the strike prices of the switch spread or straddle being placed. Although this sounds like a motherhood and apple pie statement it is not. For example a switch straddle should have the underlying price close to the strike while for a vertical call debit spread the underlying price should be above the midway point between two adjacent strikes.
3. Use options and single stock futures on stocks with volatility at the extremes (high or low) in their volatility cycle.
4. Use spreads and straddles whose options have a high implied volatility compared to the volatility of the underlying.

5. Construct the short leg(s) of the spread with options that have between six and ten weeks to expiration.
6. The single stock future must be at, or close to, fair market value.

Switch spreads have the following advantages over their equivalent debit option spreads.
- Greater profit potential.
- Risk management is easier because the switch spread is profitable over a greater price range.
- Time decay is not a factor.
- High volatility stocks provide greater profit potential.
- Volatility skews toward the long leg have no affect on profitability.
- Under certain circumstances, an option with a low implied volatility can offer attractive profit potential.

Switch spreads have two main disadvantages:
- There is unlimited potential loss that must be managed through position management considerations.
- The margin requirements of a switch spread are usually higher than the equivalent option spread. This is the result of the twenty percent margin required for a single stock future.

The option strategies discussed are the calendar spread, the long call condor spread, long straddles, the long vertical call debit spread, strangles, butterfly spreads, iron butterfly spreads, condors and box spreads. Position management and risk considerations are discussed for each option strategy.

Actual Reward/Risk Ratio: The actual reward/risk ratio is the result of a particular trade as opposed to the theoretical reward/risk ratio of a position before it is opened. This is a useful statistic for positions, such as a long straddle, with unlimited potential gains. See reward/risk ratio.

Actual Order: Either a stop/limit order or a stop at market order that is placed below (for long positions) or above (for short positions) the current market price of a stock. As opposed to a mental order, it is physically entered as a working order (opposite of a mental order).

American Style Option: An option that can be exercised by the holder at any time between purchase and expiration.

Arbitrage: Arbitrage is the process of locking-in a guaranteed small profit by taking advantage of a temporary imbalance in prices. This is accomplished by purchasing and selling the same security, or equivalent securities, at different prices so that a guaranteed profit is locked-in.

At-The-Money (ATM): An option with a strike price that is the same as or very close to, the price of the underlying stock.

ATM: See At-The-Money.

Close a Position: The opposite of opening a position. Closing a position relieves the person who opened the position from any obligations and risks association with the position being closed. It also means any future gains, including dividends, are no longer possible.

Close a Spread: When you close a spread you buy and sell in reverse order in which the spread was opened. For example if a position was opened by buying an XYZ 50 December call and selling an XYZ 55 December call the position would be closed by buy the XYX December 55 call and selling the XYZ December 50 call.

Contingent Option Order: An order to buy or sell an option based on the price of the underlying security. For example, a contingent order for IBM with a current market price of 89.55 might be: buy 10 IBM March 95 calls at market when the price of IBM reaches 91.05. This order would not be filled unless the price of IBM reaches the contingent price of 91.05.

Credit Spread: A spread in which the cash in from the sale of the short positions is greater than the cash out for the purchase of the long positions.

Day Order: A day order that has not been filled prior to close is canceled at the end of the trading day.

Debit Spread: A spread in which the cash out for the long positions is greater than the cash in from the sale of the short positions.

Delta: A measure of how much the price of an option changes when the price of the underlying stock changes.

Downdraft: A sudden, large, unexpected downturn in the price of a stock.

Down Tick: A situation where the last selling price is less than the previous selling price.

European Style Option: An option that can be exercised only on its expiration date.
Exercise price: see strike price.

Exercise: The owner of an option or single stock future "exercises" the right to own the underlying stock when the seller of the option or SSF is asked to deliver the stock.

Expected Volatility: The forecast of an individual investor. It is what an individual investor expects the volatility to be in the future. This value is based on the analysis of an individual investor.

Expiration Date: The date on which the option of buying or selling the underlying stock ends or expires.

Expiry: In the United Kingdom and other countries outside the United States expiry is used instead of expiration date.

Fill-Or-Kill: A fill-or-kill order is either executed as soon as it hits the floor or else it is canceled.

Gamma: Represents the rate of change (mathematically the first partial derivative) of delta when the underlying changes.

Gain/Loss Ratio: See reward/risk ratio.

Gain/Risk Ratio: See reward/risk ratio.

Gamma of the Gamma: A measure of how much gamma changes when the price of the underlying stock changes. (The second partial derivative of Delta)

Good-Til-Cancel: A good-til-cancel (GTC) order is either filled during the day it is placed or carried over from day-to-day until it is physically cancelled by the trader who placed it.

GTC: See Good-Til-Cancel.

Historical Volatility: Historical volatility measures the tendency of a particular stock to make large percentage movements based on price movements over a specific period of time in the past. Mathematically, historical volatility is defined as the annualized standard deviation of the percentage moves of the underlying stock price. Historical volatility is applied to the underlying stock.

Implied Volatility: A computed value that matches the theoretical price of an option with its current market price. Implied volatility is applied to options.

In-The-Money (ITM): A call option with a strike price less than (more than for a put) the price of the underlying stock.

Initial Protective Stop (IPS): The price at which the trade will be closed if things do not go as expected. An IPS represents the maximum amount you are willing to lose on a trade if you are incorrect and the trade goes against you immediately.

Initial Time Stop: The length of time that will be permitted to pass before closing an open position due to failure to move in the expected direction.

IPS: See Initial Protective Stop.

ITM: See In-The-Money.

Kappa: See Vega.

Lambda: See Vega

Leg (of a spread or straddle): A spread is composed of two or more options. Each option position is sometimes called a leg.

Legging into a Spread: Separately purchasing or selling each option in a spread.

Lift a spread: See close a spread.

Long: A stock, option or SSF that is purchased with the expectation of an increase in its value.

Market-On-Open: A market-on-open is placed in a queue and is executed after the open at a price within the opening range as soon as it reaches the front of the queue.

Mental Order: A mental order is not placed ahead of time. Instead, the trader carefully watches a stock and than places the order to buy or sell when the stock hits a certain level, (opposite of an actual order).

Net Spread Order: A net spread order might be: buy 10 MSFT March 25 calls and sell 10 MSFT March 30 calls for a net debit of 2.35. This order would not be filled unless the combination sale and purchase would generate a net debit of 2.35 or less.

OCO: See One-Cancels-Other.

Offsetting a Position: The term offsetting is the term most often used for taking off or closing a single stock future position.

One-Cancels-Other Order (OCO): This order is placed when a breakout is expected with the direction uncertain. Simultaneous buy long and sell short orders are placed. The buy long order is placed above the current market price and the sell short order is placed below the current market price. If the stock goes up the buy long order is executed. This action automatically cancels the sell short order. The filling of one order automatically cancels the other order, hence the name one-cancels-other or OCO.

Open a Position: The initial purchase or sale of a stock, option or SSF.

Open a Spread: The process of initially buying and selling the options constituting a spread is called or the spread.

Option Spread: a spread composed of options.

OTM: See Out-Of-The-Money.

Out-Of-The-Money (OTM) – A call option with a stroke price greater than (less than for a put) the price of the underlying.

Parity: A situation in which the strike price plus the premium is equal to the price of the underlying.

Placing a Spread: See open a spread.

Potential Problem Areas: Potential problem areas are determined before a trade is opened and represents an investor's estimate of prices or times where a trend could slow down or reverse.

Rho: A measure of the change in price of an option price relative to changes in the Risk Free Interest Rate.

Setup: The setup provides perspective to help place current events in the proper perspective. As such the set up forms the basis for identifying a trigger event and subsequent position management activities. It is always completed before a trading session begins.

Short: A stock, option or SSF that is sold without having ownership of the stock option or SSF. The expectation is the stock, option or SSF will decrease in value.

Putting on a Spread: See open a spread

Reward/Loss Ratio: See reward/risk ratio.

Reward/Risk Ratio: The maximum gain from a spread divided by the maximum loss from the spread. A theoretical number calculated before the spread is opened. See actual reward/risk ratio.

Single Stock Future: A future on a stock. A single stock future is considered at "fair value" when its price is consistent with the theoretical formula: SSF price = stock price x (1 + annualized interest rate - dividend).

Slippage: The difference between the price of the stock at which the order was entered and the price actually paid for the stock. Slippage can also refer to the time taken to fill an order after it has been place.

Spread: In options trading, applies to a position containing two or more options on the same underlying stock. In futures trading, "spread" refers to futures contracts on two different, but correlated, underlying securities or indexes.

SSF: Abbreviation for a single stock future.

Switch Spread: a spread that is the equivalent of an option spread except it contains at least one SSF on the same underlying stock.

Strike Price: The price at which the owner of an option contract can buy (a call) or sell (a put) the underlying stock.

Take Off a Spread: see close a spread.

Theta: Measure the affect of the passage of time on the price of an option.

Time Cancel: The length of time to leave an unexecuted opening order as a working order before canceling it.

Time Decay: The longer a call option has to expiration, the more time it has to increase in value. Therefore, at any given stock price, a long-term call sells for more than a short-term call. Furthermore, an option's time value decreases to zero at expiration. This is called time decay.

Trailing Protective Stop: Either a mental or actual stop order that is made with the intent of protecting some of the profit already generated. It is called a trailing stop because it trails the price of the stock as it moves in your direction. The purpose of trailing protective stops is to prevent a winning trade from becoming a losing trade.

Trigger Event: A trigger event is some predetermined action or trading situation that will make you "pull the trigger" and open a trading position. The key word is "predetermined."

Underlying Stock: The stock or index upon which an option or single stock future is based.

Up Tick: A situation where the last selling price is greater than the previous selling price.

Vega: A measure of the sensitivity of the option price relative to the change in the stock's volatility. The Black-Scholes model uses historical volatility to determine an option's fair price.

Whipsawed: A situation in which an actual protective stop order is prematurely triggered by a fleeting, temporary down tick. The result is the trader is taken out of a long (or short) position in the middle of the up trend (downtrend) and thereby leaves additional profits on the table.

Working Order: An order to buy or sell that has been confirmed as received but has not been filled.

Zeta: Measures the percentage change in option price per 1% change in implied volatility.

Option and stock characteristics that are different from futures contracts are in bold.

- The buyer of an option has the right to demand delivery of the underlying stock anytime before the expiration date. The same is true for a futures contract.
- **The buyer of a futures contract has the obligation to take delivery of the stock at expiration.** The option purchaser does not have this obligation.
- For a limited period of time, the sale of an option contract creates an obligation to deliver the underlying stock upon demand. The same is true for a futures contract.
- **A future is considered at "fair value" when its price is consistent with the theoretical formula:**
  Fair Value = stock price x (1 + annualized interest rate - dividend).
- **For a futures contract, the market price and the theoretical price are usually very close to one another.** All of the variables in the formula for the price of a futures contract are a question of fact and can be determined. Therefore, when a futures contract is not at or near the fair market value, either wait for arbitrage to correct the situation or check the assumptions about either the interest rate or the dividends. This is not the case for options. Theoretical prices and market prices are often different because the option formula has one variable, volatility of the underlying, which can be estimated in a statistical probability sense only.
- Both implied volatility and the volatility of the underlying have a major impact on the price of an option. **The term implied volatility has no meaning in relation to the price of a futures contract because the volatility of the underlying has no impact on the price of a futures contract.** (See the formula for the fair market value of a futures contract.)
- Time decay can become a major consideration for some option spreads. **A futures contract does not experience time decay.** (See the formula for the fair market value of a futures contract.)
- **Once the fair value is determined, the future has a delta close to or equal to 1.0.**
- **A futures contract can be shorted on a down tick. A stock cannot.**
- **A future can be shorted without borrowing the stock. A stock cannot.**
- **A single stock future has a twenty percent margin requirement.** Compare this to stocks with a twenty-five percent margin for pattern day traders and a fifty percent margin requirement for trades that are open more than one day.
- For any given underlying security, there are option alternatives with different strike prices and different expiration dates. **There may be futures contracts with different expiration dates, however, the prices are usually close to the underlying price and for each expiration date there is only one price, the fair value.**
- **Shorting a futures contract does not create a credit to your account.**

REFERENCES

"Active Trader's Online Brokerage Guide" [2004]. *Active Trader.* 5, 10, 28-41. (October).
Extensive list of online brokers with considerable detail about each broker.

Allure, Marc [2003]. *The Option Strategist.* New York: McGraw-Hill.

Angell, George. [1983]. *Sure Thing Options Trading.* New York: Penguin Group.

Ansbacher, Max [2000]. *The New Options Market 4th Edition.* New York: John Wiley & Sons.

Apostolou, Nick and Barbara Apostolou [2000]. *Keys to Investing in Options and Futures 3rd Edition.* Hauppauge, NY: Barron's Press.

Bernstein, Jake and Elliot Bernstein [2002]. *Stock Market Strategies That Work.* New York: McGraw-Hill
Five Reasons to Keep Things Simple. Position Management.

Bernstein, Jake [2003]. *How to Trade the New Single Stock Futures.* Chicago: Dearborn Trade Publishing.

Bernstein, Jake [1998]. *The Compleat Day Trader II.* New York: McGraw-Hill.

Bigalow, Steve [2004]. *Market Timing with Candlesticks.* Technical Analysis of Stocks and Commodities, 22, 5, pp. 88-90.

Bigalow, Steven W. [2002]. *Profitable Candlestick Trading.* New York: John Wiley & Sons.

Bittman, James B. [1997]. *Options for the Stock Investor.* New York: McGraw-Hill.

Bollinger, John [2002]. *Bollinger on Bollinger Bands.* New York: McGraw-Hill.

Brach, Marion A. [2003]. *Real Options in Practice.* New York: John Wiley & Sons.
Different viewpoint on volatility, time decay and option pricing models such as Black-Scholes. Traders familiar with mathematical game theory and binomial decision trees will find this a must read for an alternative approach to option pricing.

Brown, Constance [2002]. *All About Technical Analysis.* New York: McGraw-Hill.

Brown, Constance [1999]. *Technical Analysis for the Trading Professional.* New York: McGraw-Hill.

Bulkowski, Thomas N. [2002]. *Trading Classic Chart Patterns.* New York: John Wiley & Sons.
pp. 69-70 Protect a profit, minimize a loss, time loss, maximize your use of capital.

Bulkowski, Thomas N. [2000]. *Encyclopedia of Chart Patterns.* New York: John Wiley & Sons.

Caplan, David L [1995]. *The New Options Advantage Revised Edition.* New York: McGraw-Hill.
Trading plan pp 149 – 174, money management pp. 163-164.

Cassidy, Donald L. *It's When You Sell That Counts.* New York: McGraw-Hill.

Chande, Tushar S. [2001]. *Beyond Technical Analysis 3rd Edition.* New York: John Wiley & Sons.

Colby, Robert and Thomas Meyers [2002]. *Encyclopedia of Market Indicators.* New York: McGraw-Hill.

Copeland, Tom and Vladimir Antikarov [2001]. *Real Options: A Practical Guide.* New York: Texere, LLC.
For advanced traders only. Simple algebra and bi-nodal decision trees combined with present value and Bayesian analysis. If you do not have a good understanding of the terms in the previous sentence, then this book is not for you. For people who are comfortable with these concepts, this is an excellent book...a must have.

Crask, Mitch [2004]. "Reply to Margin Question [Crask 2003] In Your Letters." *Stocks, Futures, Options,* 3, 2 (February), p.12.

First use of the term switch spread. Explains the difference between a margin requirement and net debit for a debit spread.

Crask, Mitch [2003]. "Single Stock Futures Add a New Twist to Options Play." *Stocks, Futures, Options,* 2, 11 (November), pp. 42-46.

Coyle, Brian [2000]. *Currency Options.* Chicago: AMACOM.

Dalton, John M. [2001]. *How the Stock Market Works 3rd Edition.* New York: New York Institute of Finance.

Market and transaction mechanics.

Dicks, James [2004]. *FOREX Made Easy: 6 Ways to Trade the Dollar.* New York: McGraw-Hill. Excellent introduction to trading currencies.

Dobson, Edward D. (1985) Understanding Fibonacci Numbers. Greenville, SC: Traders Press, Inc.

Dorsey, Thomas, J. *Point and Figure Charting 2nd Edition.* New York: John Wiley & Sons. Excellent book on point and figure charting.

Edwards, Robert D. and John Magee [2001]. *Technical Analysis of Stock Trends 8th Edition.* New York: AMACOM.

Eng, William F. [1993]. *The Day Trader's Manual.* New York: John Wiley & Sons.

Eng, William F. [1988]. *Technical Analysis of Stocks, Options and Futures.* New York: McGraw-Hill.

Evans, Richard E [2000]. *The Index Fund Solution.* New York: Simon & Schuster.

Farrell, C.A. [1999]. *Day Trader Online.* New York: John Wiley & Sons. Bid/Ask specialist.

Ferri, Richard A. [200]. *All About Index Funds.* New York: McGraw-Hill

Fine, Robert E. and Robert B. Feduniak [1988]. *Futures Trading: Concepts and Strategies.* New York: New York Institute of Finance.

Fischer, Robert [2001]. *The New Fibonacci Trader Workbook.* New York: John Wiley & Sons.

Fischer, Robert [1993]. *Fibonacci Applications and Strategies for Traders.* New York: John Wiley & Sons.

Frost, Alfred J. and Robert Prechter, Jr. [1999]. *Elliott Wave Principle.* New York: John Wiley & Sons.

Fontanills, George and Tom Gentile [2003]. *The Volatility Course.* New York: John Wiley & Sons. Emphasizes volatility as a market tool. Examines and explains every aspect of volatility and the importance of volatility to option trading. Provides trading strategies under a variety of situations. Covers how to quantify volatility, strategies based on volatility and strategies for high and low volatility markets.

Fontanills, George A [1998]. *The Options Course.* New York: John Wiley & Sons. Excellent introduction to options. Clearly written in small, easy-to-learn steps.

Fontanills, George A. [1998]. *The Options Course Workbook: Step-By-Step Exercises and Tests to Help You Master the Options Course.* New York: John Wiley & Sons. The title says it all. An excellent workbook that teaches how to apply the concepts in the companion text.

Fosback, Norman G. [1994]. *Stock Market Logic.* Chicago: Dearborn Press.

Gallacher, William R. [1999]. *The Options Edge.* New York: McGraw-Hill. A book for intermediate and above option traders who want to eliminate all the complexity surrounding option analysis and trading.

REFERENCES

Gallea, Anthony M. [2002]. *Bulls Make Money – Bears Make Money – Pigs Get Slaughtered.* New York: New York Institute of Finance.

Gidel, Susan A. [2000]. *Stock Index Futures and Options.* New York: John Wiley & Sons.

Gonzalez, F. and W. Rhee [1999]. *Strategies for the Online Day Trader.* New York: McGraw-Hill.

Graham, Benjamin and David L. Dodd [1996]. *Security Analysis: The Classic 1934 Edition.* New York: McGraw-Hill.

Greenberg, Steven A. [2001]. *Single Stock Futures: The Complete Guide.* Greenville, SC: Traders Press, Inc.

Guppy, Daryl [1997]. *Market Trading Tactics.* New York: John Wiley & Sons.

Harris, L [1986]. "A Transaction Data Study of Weekly and Intraday Patterns in Stock Returns." Journal of Financial Economics, 16, 99-117.

Hobbs, Derrik S. [2003]. *Fibonacci for the Active Trader.* Los Angeles, CA: TradingMarkets.

Hoggart, V.E., Jr. and Majorie Bicknell-Johnson [1979]. "Reflections Across Two and Three Glass Panes." The Fibonacci Quarterly, 17, (April), 118-142

Hull, John G. [2003]. *Options, Futures and Other Derivatives. 5th Edition.* New York: Prentice-Hall.

Covers derivative markets and risk management. Assumes a basic knowledge of finance, statistics and probability. No prior knowledge of options, futures, and swaps. Requires quantitative skills.

Isaacman, Max [2000]. *How to Be an Index Investor.* New York: McGraw-Hill.

Jenkins, Michael S. [1992]. *The Geometry of Stock Market Profits.* Greenville, SC: Traders Press, Inc.

Chapter Nine on options is one of the best discussions of the practical aspects of trading options. Excellent book for position and risk management and the geometry of trading including proportion and harmony, and impulse waves.

Kaufman, Perry J. [1998]. *Trading Systems and Methods 3rd Edition.* New York: John Wiley & Sons.

Position Management

Lafferty, Patrick [2002]. *Single Stock Futures.* New York: McGraw-Hill.

Leizman, Jon [2002]. *Short-Term Trading, Long-Term Profits.* New York: McGraw-Hill.

Overnight trades, trading strategies, trade mechanics, daily routine, bibliography.

Lerman, David. [2001]. *Exchange Traded Funds and the E-mini Stock Index Futures.* New York: John Wiley & Sons.

Lofton, Todd [2001]. *Getting Started In Futures 4th Edition.* New York: John Wiley & Sons.

Luca, Cornelius [1997]. *Technical Analysis Applications in the Global Currency Markets.* New York: New York Institute of Finance.

Lukeman, Josh [2000]. *The Market Maker's Edge.* New York: McGraw-Hill.

McClatchy, Will [2003]. *Index Funds.* New York: John Wiley & Sons.

McClean, William [2003]. "Timing Events with the Calendar Spread." Active Trader, 9, 10 (October), pp. 66-67.

McMillan, Lawrence G. [2002]. *Options as a Strategic Investment. 4th Edition.* New York: New York Institute of Finance.

McMillan, Lawrence G. [2002]. *Profit with Options.* New York: John Wiley & Sons.

McMillan, Lawrence G. [1996]. *McMillan on Options.* New York: John Wiley & Sons.

Marlow, Jerry [2001]. *Option Pricing: Black-Scholes Made Easy.* New York: John Wiley & Sons. An excellent, simple, easy to understand visual presentation of Black-Scholes in PowerPoint® format. An interactive, animated, option pricing tutorial on CD ROM is included.

Mendoza, Alex [2004]. "Put/Call Parity." Technical Analysis of Stocks and Commodities. 27, 6 (June), pp. 64.66.

Merrill, Arthur [1983]. *M & W Wave Patterns.* Chappaqua NY: Analysis Press.

Morris, Gregory L. [1992]. *Candlestick Charting Explained.* Chicago: Irwin Professional Publishing.

Murphy, John [2002]. *Technical Analysis of the Financial Markets 2nd Edition.* New York: Putnam Press.

Neal, Jeff [2003]. "Calendar Ratio Backspread." Technical Analysis of Stocks and Commodities, 21, 10 (October), pp. 58-61.

Nison, Steve [2001]. *Japanese Candlestick Charting Techniques 2nd Edition.* New York: New York Institute of Finance

Nison, Steve [1994]. *Beyond Candlesticks.* New York: John Wiley & Sons.

Options Institute, The (Ed.) [1999]. *Options: Essential Concepts & Trading Strategies 3rd Edition.* New York: McGraw-Hill.

How market makers trade pp. 253-273. The predictive power of options pp. 357-388.

Paulos, John A. [2003]. *A Mathematician Plays the Stock Market.* New York: Basic Books.

Pierce, Phillips [1982]. *The Dow Jones Averages 1885 – 1980.* Homewood, IL: Dow Jones – Irwin.

Prechter, Jr., Robert T. "Fibonacci-Based Fractal Form and Elliott Waves." Technical Analysis of Stocks and Commodities. 21, 9 (September), 74-77.

Pring, Martin J. [2003]. *Technician's Guide to Day and Swing Trading.* New York: McGraw-Hill.

Pring, Martin J. [2002]. *Technical Analysis Explained 4th Edition.* New York: McGraw-Hill. Compendium on technical analysis.

Pring, Martin J. [2002]. *How to Select Stocks Using Technical Analysis.* New York: McGraw-Hill.

Pring Martin J. [2002]. *Candlesticks Explained.* New York: McGraw-Hill.

Roth, Harrison [1994]. *LEAPS.* Chicago: Irwin. Covers equity options over a period of one to three years.

Schlossberg, Boris [2004]. "What Happened To My Stop Loss?" *Stocks Futures & Options.* 3,1 (January), pp. 121 –122.

Seyler, Jeffrey P. [2004]. "Better Returns with Single Stock Futures." *Technical Analysis of Stocks and Commodities*, 22, 5 (May), pp. 84-86.

Sheimo, Michael D. [1999]. *Stock Market Rules.* New York: McGraw-Hill.

Stevens, Leigh [2002]. *Essential Technical Analysis.* New York: John Wiley & Sons. Fibonacci pp. 129-131, Gann pp. 309-319, Elliott Wave pp. 319-329.

Summa, John F. and Jonathan W. Lubow [2002]. *Options on Futures.* New York: John Wiley & Sons. A how-to guide for options on futures. Each strategy is explained with hypothetical examples and reconstruction of actual trades.

References

Taylor, France [2000]. *Mastering Derivative Markets 2nd Edition.* New York: Prentice-Hall.
> Excellent overview plus chapters on risk management and accounting for derivatives.

"Traders' Resource: Data Services" [2004]. *Technical Analysis of Stocks & Commodities.* <u>22</u>, 11, (November).
> Extensive list of data services.

Trester, Kenneth R. [2002]. *The Complete Options Player 4th Edition.* Lake Tahoe, NY: Institute for Options Research.

"Traders' Resource: Data Services" [2004]. *Technical Analysis of Stocks & Commodities.* <u>22</u>, 11, (November).

Veale, Stuart R. [2001]. *Stocks, Bonds, Options, Futures. 2nd Edition.* New York: New York Institute of Finance.
> Excellent overview of derivatives mentioned in title. Also includes trade execution, back office operations and global investing.

Velez, Oliver and Greg Capra [2000]. *Tools and Tactics for the Master Day Trader.* New York: McGraw-Hill.
> Position Management.

Wasendorf, Russell [2004]. *The Complete Guide to Single Stock Futures.* New York: McGraw-Hill.
> Nothing has been left out. The book is, indeed, complete.

Wheelan, Alexander H. [1989]. *Study Helps in Point and Figure Technique.* Burlington VT: Fraser Publishing.
> Reprint of original 1947 book.

Williams, Michael S., and Amy Hoffman [2001]. *Fundamentals of the Options Market.* New York: McGraw-Hill.
> Appendix A has a summary of order types. Appendix B has a summary of most option strategies. Appendix C has the various expiration cycles.

Zelkin, Marvin H. [2002]. *It's Your Option: A Trader's Primer.* Greenville, SC: Traders Press, Inc.

Online Brokers

"Active Trader's Online Brokerage Guide" [2004]. *Active Trader.* 5, 10, 28-41. (October).
> Extensive list of online brokers with considerable detail about each broker.

Charting Services

"Traders' Resource: Data Services" [2004]. *Technical Analysis of Stocks & Commodities.* 22, 11, (November).
> Extensive list of data services.

Journals Listed Alphabetically

Active Trader

  Active Trader Magazine

  P.O. Box 567

  Mt. Morris, IL 61054-0567

  (800)341-9384

  www.activetradermag.com

  Available in most major bookstores and newsstands and by subscription.

Futures

  P.O. Box 2122

  Skokie, IL 60076-7822

  (888)-804-6612

  www.futures.com

  Available in most bookstores and newsstands and by subscription.

SFO: Stocks Futures Options

  Wassendorf & Associates

  P.O. Box 849

  Cedar Falls, IA 50613

  www.sfomag.com

  Available in bookstores and newsstands in financial areas and by subscription.

Technical Analysis of Stocks & Commodities

  (800)832-4642

  E-mail: circ@traders.com

  www.traders.com

  Available in most bookstores and newsstands and by subscription.

Tradersworld

  Halliker's, Inc.

  2508 Grayrock St.

  Springfield, MO 65810

  www.tradersworld.com

  Available in most bookstores and newsstands and by subscription.

Partial List of Publications of Traders Press, Inc.®

A Complete Guide to Trading Profits (Paris)
A Professional Look at S&P Day Trading (Trivette)
A Treasury of Wall Street Wisdom (Editors: Schultz & Coslow)
Beginner's Guide to Computer Assisted Trading (Alexander)
Channels and Cycles: A Tribute to J.M. Hurst (Millard)
Chart Reading for Professional Traders (Jenkins)
Comparison of Twelve Technical Trading Systems (Lukac, Brorsen, & Irwin)
Complete Stock Market Trading and Forecasting Course (Jenkins)
Cyclic Analysis (J.M. Hurst)
Dynamic Trading (Miner)
Essentials of Trading: It's Not WHAT You Think, It's HOW You Think (Pesavento)
Exceptional Trading: The Mind Game (Roosevelt)
Fibonacci Ratios with Pattern Recognition (Pesavento)
Futures Spread Trading: The Complete Guide (Smith)
Geometry of Markets (Gilmore)
Geometry of Stock Market Profits (Jenkins)
Harmonic Vibrations (Pesavento)
How to Trade in Stocks (Livermore & Smitten)
Hurst Cycles Course (J.M. Hurst)
Investing by the Stars (Weingarten)
Investor Skills Training: Managing Emotions and Risk in the Market (Ronin)
It's Your Option (Zelkin)
Keeping a Cool Head in a Hot Market (Roosevelt)
Magic of Moving Averages (Lowry)
Market Beaters (Collins)
Market Rap: The Odyssey of a Still-Struggling Commodity Trader (Collins)
Overcoming 7 Deadly Sins of Trading (Roosevelt)
Planetary Harmonics of Speculative Markets (Pesavento)
Point & Figure Charting (Aby)
Point & Figure Charting: Commodity and Stock Trading Techniques (Zieg)
Precision Trading with Stevenson Price and Time Targets (J.R. Stevenson)
Private Thoughts From a Trader's Diary (Pesavento & MacKay)
Profitable Patterns for Stock Trading (Pesavento)
RoadMap to the Markets (Busby)
RSI: The Complete Guide (Hayden)
Stock Patterns for Day Trading (2 volumes) (Rudd)
Technically Speaking (Wilkinson)
Technical Trading Systems for Commodities and Stocks (Patel)
The Amazing Life of Jesse Livermore: World's Greatest Stock Trader (Smitten)
The Handbook of Global Securities Operations (O'Connell & Steiniger)
The Opening Price Principle: The Best Kept Secret on Wall Street (Pesavento & MacKay)
The Professional Commodity Trader (Kroll)
The Taylor Trading Technique (Taylor)
*The Trading Rule That Can Make You Rich** (Dobson)
Top Traders Under Fire (Collins)
Trading Secrets of the Inner Circle (Goodwin)
Trading S&P Futures and Options (Lloyd)
Twelve Habitudes of Highly Successful Traders (Roosevelt)
Understanding Bollinger Bands (Dobson)
Understanding Eminis: Trading to Win (Williams)
Understanding Fibonacci Numbers (Dobson)
Winning Edge 4 (Toghraie)
Winning Market Systems (Appel)